PREFACE TO SECOND EDITION.

In preparing The Psychical Correlation of Religious Emotion and Sexual Desire for its second edition, the author has incorporated in it a considerable amount of additional evidence in support of his theory. He has carefully verified all references; he has endeavored to eliminate all unnecessary material; and, finally, he has changed the style of the work by dividing it into three parts, thus greatly simplifying the text. He feels under many obligations to his critics, both to those who thought his little book worthy of commendation, and to those who deemed his premises and conclusions erroneous. He feels grateful to the former, because they have caused him to believe that he has added somewhat to the literature of science; he thanks the latter, because in pointing out that which they considered untrue, they have forced him to a new and more searching study of the questions involved, thereby strengthening his belief in the truthfulness of his conclusions.

To the second edition of The Psychical Correlation of Religious Emotion and Sexual Desire, the author has seen fit to add certain other essays. In preparing these essays for publication, he has borrowed freely from his published papers, therefore, he desires to thank the publishers of the New York Medical Record, Century Magazine, Denver Medical Times, Charlotte Monthly and American Naturalist for granting him permission to use such of his published material (belonging to them) as he saw fit.

The author asks the indulgence of the reader for certain repetitions in the text. These have not been occasioned by any lack of data, but occur simply because he believes that an argument is rendered stronger and more convincing by the frequent use of the same data whenever and wherever it is possible to use them. When this plan is followed, the reader, so the author believes, becomes familiar with the author's line of thought, and is, consequently, better able to comprehend and appreciate his meaning.

Finally, the author has been led to the publication of these essays by a firm belief in the truthfulness of the propositions advanced therein. He may *not live to see these propositions accepted, yet he believes that, in the future, perhaps, in worthier and more able hands, they will be so weightily and forcibly elaborated and advanced that their verity will be universally acknowledged.*

"Waveland," September 17, 1897.

CONTENTS.

Religion and Lust
    Chap. I. The Origin of Religious Feeling
    Chap. II. Phallic Worship
    Chap. III. The Psychical Correlation of Religious Emotion and Sexual Desire
Viraginity and Effemination
Borderlands and Crankdom
Genius and Degeneration
The Effect of Female Suffrage on Posterity
Is It the Beginning of the End?

CHAPTER I.
THE ORIGIN OF RELIGIOUS FEELING.

I believe that man originated his first ideas of the supernatural from the external phenomena of nature which were perceptible to one or more of his five senses; his first theogony was a natural one and one taken directly from nature. In ideation the primal bases of thought must have been founded, *ab initio*, upon sensual perceptions; hence, must have been materialistic and natural. Spencer, on the contrary, maintains that in man, "the first traceable conception of a supernatural being is the conception of a ghost."[1]

Primitive man's struggle for existence was so very severe that his limited sagacity was fully occupied in obtaining food and shelter; many thousands of years must have passed away before he evolved any idea of weapons other than stones and clubs. When he arrived at a psychical acuteness that originated traps, spears, bows and arrows, his struggle for existence became easier and he had leisure to notice the various natural phenomena by which he was surrounded. Man evolved a belief in a god long before he arrived at a conception of a ghost, double, or soul. He soon discovered that his welfare was mainly dependent on nature, consequently he began to propitiate nature, and finally ended by creating a system of theogony founded on nature alone.[A]

"It is an evident historical fact that man *first personified natural phenomena*, and then made use of these personifications to personify his own inward acts, his psychical ideas and conceptions. This was the necessary process, and external idols were formed before those which were internal and peculiar to himself."[2] Sun, moon, and star; mountain, hill, and dale; torrent, waterfall, and rill, all became to him distinct personalities, powerful beings, that might do him great harm or much good. He therefore endeavored to propitiate them, just as a dog endeavors to get the good will of man by abjectly crawling toward him on his belly and licking his feet. There was no element of true worship in the propitiatory offerings of primitive man; in the beginning he was essentially a materialist—he became a spiritualist later on. Man's first religion must have been, necessarily, a material one; he worshiped (propitiated) only that which he could see, or feel, or hear, or touch; his undeveloped psychical being could grasp nothing higher; his limited understanding could not frame an idea involving a spiritual element such as animism undoubtedly presents. Apropos of the dream birth of the soul, all terrestrial mammals dream, and in some of them, notably the dog and monkey, an observer can almost predicate the subject of their dreams by watching their actions while they are under dream influence; yet no animal save man, as far as we know, has ever evolved any idea of ghost or soul.[B] It may be said, on the other hand, that since animals show, unmistakably, that they are, in a measure, fully conscious of certain phenomena in the economy of nature, and while I am not prepared to state that any element of worship enters into their regard, I yet believe that an infinitesimal increase in the development of their psychical beings would, undoubtedly, lead some of them to a natural religion such as our pithecoid ancestors practiced.

The Egyptians noticed, over four thousand years ago, that cynocephali, the dog-headed apes of the Nile Valley, were in the habit of welcoming the rising sun with dancing and with howls of joy! "The habit of certain monkeys (cynocephali) assembling, as it were, in full court, and chattering noisily at sunrise and sunset, would almost justify the, as yet, uncivilized Egyptians in intrusting them with the charge of hailing the god morning and evening as he appeared in the east or passed away in the west."[3] An English fox-terrier of my acquaintance is very much afraid of thunder or any noise simulating thunder. A load of coal rushing through a chute into the coal cellar will send him, trembling and alarmed, to his hiding-place beneath a bed. This dog has never been shot over, nor has he, as far as I know, ever heard the sound of a gun. I am confident that he considers the thunder as being supernatural, and that he would propitiate it, if he only knew how.

It is not probable that, at the present time, there exists a race of people which has not formulated an idea of ghost or soul; yet in ancient times, and up to a century or so ago, there existed many peoples who had not conceived any idea of ghosts or doubles.

According to Maspero, Sayce, Champollion, and other Egyptologists, the ancient Egyptians probably had a natural theogony long before they arrived at any idea of a double. In the beginning they treated the double or ghost with scant ceremony; it was only after many years that an element of worship entered into their treatment of the ghosts of their dead ancestors. They believed, at first, that the double dwelt forever in the tomb along with the dead body; afterward, they evolved the idea that the double of the dead man journeyed to the "Islands of the Blessed," where it was judged by Osiris according to its merits.[4] We have no reason for believing that the ancient Hebrews at the time of the Exodus had any knowledge of, or belief in, the existence of the soul or double, yet, that they did believe in the supernatural can not be questioned.[C] When Cook touched at Tierra del Fuego, he found a people in whom there existed mental habitudes but little above those to be found in the anthropoid apes. They had no knowledge whatever of the soul or double and but a dim concept of the powers of nature; they had not yet advanced far enough in psychical development to evolve any consistent form of natural theogony. They had only a shadowy concept of evil beings, powers of the air that inhabited the dense brakes of the forest, whom it would be dangerous to molest. Father Junipero Serra declares that when he first established the Mission Dolores, the Ahwashtees, Ohlones, Romanos, Altahmos, Tuolomos, and other Californian tribes had no word in their language for god, ghost, or devil.[5] The Inca Yupangui informed Balboa that there were many tribes in the interior which had no idea of ghost or soul.[6] Another writer says, that the Chirihuanas did not worship anything either in heaven or on earth, and that they had no belief whatever in a future state.[7] Modern travelers have, however, found distinct evidences of phallic worship in certain observances and customs of this tribe.[8]

Certain autochthons of India, when first discovered, were exceedingly immature in religious beliefs; they had neither god nor devil; they wandered through the woods subsisting on berries and fruits, and such small animals as their undeveloped and feeble sagacity allowed them to capture and slay. They did not even provide themselves with shelter, but, in pristine nakedness, roamed the forests of the Ghauts, animals but slightly above the anthropoid apes in point of intelligence. "In Central California we find," says Bancroft, "whole tribes subsisting on roots, herbs, and insects; having no boats, no clothing, no laws, no God."[9]

In the northwestern corner of the American continent there dwells a primitive race, which, for the sake of unification, I will style the Aleutians. When these people were first discovered they were in that state of social economics which they had reached after thousands of years of psychical and social evolution; a primitive people, such as our own ancestors were in the very beginning of civilization. The word civilization is used advisedly; civilization is comparative, and its degrees begin with the inception of man himself.

In their theogony, the Aleutians had arrived at an idea of the double or soul, thus showing that their religion had progressed several steps toward abstraction, that triumph of civilized religiosity; yet there remained enough veneration of natural objects to show that the origin of the religious feeling began, with them, in nature-propitiation. The bladder of the bear, which viscus, in the estimation of the Aleutians, is the seat of life, is at once suspended above the entrance of the *kachim* or communal dwelling and worshiped by the hunter who has slain the beast from which it was taken. Moreover, when the bear falls beneath the weapons of an Aleutian, the man begs pardon of the beast and prays the latter to forgive him and to do him no harm. "A hunter who has struck a mortal blow generally remains within his hut for one or several days, according to the importance of the slain animal."[10] The first herring that is caught is showered with compliments and blessings; pompous titles are lavished upon it, and it is handled with the greatest respect and reverence; it is the herring-god![11]

Sidné, chief god of the Aleutian theogony, on final analysis, is found to be the Earth, mother of all things. The *angakouts*, or priests, of this people individualize and deify, however, all the phenomena of nature; there are cloud-gods, sea-gods, river-gods, fire-gods, rain-gods, storm-gods, etc., etc., etc. Everywhere, throughout all nature, the Inoit, or Aleutian system of theology, penetrates, stripped, it is true, of much of its original materialism, yet retaining enough to show its undoubted origin in the sensual percepts, recepts, and concepts of its primal founders.

As I have observed above, the religion of these people has gained a certain degree of abstraction, and this abstraction is further shown by the presence of certain phallic rites and ceremonies in their religious observances; but of this, more anon.[D]

In most of the tribes of Equatorial Africa, nature-worship has been superseded by ghost-worship, devil-worship, or witch-worship, or, rather, by ghost, devil, or witch propitiation; yet, in the sanctity of the fetich, which is everywhere present, we see a relic of nature-worship. Moreover, many of these tribes deify natural phenomena, such as the sun, the moon, the stars, thunder, lightning, etc., etc., etc., showing that here, too, in all probability, religious feeling had its origin in nature propitiation.

Abstraction also enters, to a certain extent, into the religious beliefs of most of these negroes, in whom primal materialism has given place to the unbridled superstition of crude spiritism. The curious habit these people have of scraping a little bone dust from the skull of a dead ancestor and then eating it with their food, thus, as they think, transmitting from the dead to the living the qualities of the former, is close kin to, and, in my opinion, is probably derived from, a worship of the generative principle. When we take into consideration the fact that circumcision, *extensio clitoridis*, and other phallic rites are exceedingly common and prevalent among these negroes, this opinion has strong evidence in its support.[12]

The Wa-kamba may have some idea of immortality, though observers have never been able to determine this definitely. "The dead bodies of chiefs are not thrown to the hyenas, as with the Masai, but are carefully buried instead… The bodies of less important members of the tribe are simply thrown to the hyenas."[13]

In this people, religious ideas are exceedingly primitive and indefinite. They seem to propitiate nature, however, when they wish rain, for they offer up to the rain-spirit votive offerings of bananas, grain, and beer, which they place beneath the trees. This seems to be their only religious rite according to Gregory, who, in all probability is in error. For, in the next sentence, he informs us that these negroes practice circumcision. He thinks that they perform this operation for sanitary reasons, "as the natives have continually to ford streams and wade through swamps abounding in the larvæ of

Bilharzia hæmaturia, the rite no doubt lessens the danger of incurring hæmaturia."[14] This is bestowing upon ignorant and savage negroes a psychical acuteness which far transcends that of the laity of civilized races! What do the Wa-kamba know of sanitation, hæmaturia, and the larva of Bilharzia![E] Circumcision among these people always occurs at puberty, and is, unquestionably, a phallic rite. Parenthetically, it may be stated here that a few of the primitive peoples still in existence appear to have grasped the idea of the life-giving principle, and to have established worship of the *functio generationis* without having experienced certain preliminary psychical stages necessary for its evolution from nature-worship. I believe, however, that this is apparent and not real; nature-worship, very probably, at one time existed among all these people.

The Kikuyu have a very elaborate system of theogony, in which all of the phenomena of nature with which they are acquainted are deified. A goat is invariably sacrificed to the sun when they set out on a journey, and its blood is carried along and sprinkled on the paths and bridges in order to appease the spirits of the forest and the river.

Stuhlmann places this tribe among the Bantu; from the evidence of other observers, however, they seem to be Nilotic Hamites, and belong properly to the Masai.[15] This would account for the similarity of method in circumcision, which, among both Kikuyu and Masai, is incomplete. Johnston calls attention to this very peculiar method and describes it minutely in a Latin foot-note.[16]

The Masai are mixed devil, nature, and phallic worshipers; the last mentioned cult being evolved, beyond question, from nature-worship. It may be set down as an established fact that, where nature-worship does not exist in some form or other among primitive peoples, phallic worship is likewise absent. Indeed, such peoples generally have no religious feeling whatever. They may have some shadowy idea of an evil spirit like the *"Aurimwantya dsongo ngombe auri kinemu,"* the Old Man of the Woods[17] of the Wa-pokomo, but that is all.

Carl Lumholtz, writing of the Australians, says: "The Australian blacks do not, like many other savage tribes, attach any ideas of divinity to the sun or moon. On one of our expeditions the full moon rose large and red over the palm forest. Struck by the splendor of the scene, I pointed at the moon and asked my companions, 'Who made it?' They answered, 'Other blacks.' Thereupon I asked, 'Who made the sun?' and got the same answer. The natives also believe that they themselves can produce rain, particularly with the help of wizards. To produce rain they call *milka*. When on our expeditions we were overtaken by violent tropical storms, my blacks always became enraged at the strangers who had caused the rain."[18] In regard to their belief in the existence of a double or soul, the same author sums up as follows: "Upon the whole, it may be said that these children of nature are unable to conceive a human soul independent of the body, and the future life of the individual lasts no longer than his physical remains."[19] Mr. Mann, of New South Wales, who, according to Lumholtz, has made a thirty years' study of the Australians, says that the natives have no religion whatever, except fear of the "devil-devil."[20] Another writer, and one abundantly qualified to judge, says that they acknowledge no supreme being, have no idols, and believe only in an evil spirit whom they do not worship. They say that this spirit is afraid of fire, so they never venture abroad after dusk without a fire-stick.[21]

"I verily believe we have arrived at the sum total of their religion, if a superstitious dread of the unknown can be so designated. Their mental capacity does not admit of their grasping the higher truths of pure religion," says Eden.[22] It is simply an inherent fear of the unknown; the natural, inborn caution of thousands of years of inherited experiences.

In these savages we see a race whose psychical status is so low in the intellectual scale that they have not evolved any idea of the double or soul. The mental capacity of the Australians, I take it, is no lower than was that of any race (no matter how intellectual it may be at the present time) at one period of its history. All races have a tendency toward psychical development under favorable surroundings; it has been a progress instead of a decadence, a rise instead of a fall! Evolution has not ceased; nor will it end until *Finis* is written at the bottom of Time's last page.

There are yet other people who believe in the supernatural, yet who have no idea of immortality. When Gregory ascended the glacier of Mount Kenya, the water froze in the cooking-pots which had been filled over night. His carriers were terribly alarmed by the phenomenon, and swore that the water was bewitched! The explorer scolded them for their silliness and bade them set the pots on the fire, which, having been done, "the men sat round and anxiously watched; when it melted they joyfully told me that the demon was expelled, and I told them they could now use the water; but as soon as my back was turned they poured it away, and refilled their pots from the adjoining brook."[23]

Stanley declares that no traces of religious feeling can be found in the Wahuma. "They believe most thoroughly in the existence of an evil influence in the form of a man, who exists in uninhabited places, as a wooded, darksome gorge, or large extent of reedy brake, but that he can be propitiated by gifts; therefore the lucky hunter leaves a portion of the meat, which he tosses, however, as he would to a dog, or he places an egg, or a small banana, or a kid-skin, at the door of the miniature dwelling, which is always at the entrance to the zeriba."[24]

This observer shows that he does not know the true meaning of the word religion; the example that he gives demonstrates the fact that these negroes *do* have religious feeling. The simple act of offering propitiatory gifts to the "evil influence" is, from the very nature of the deed, a religious observance. Furthermore, these savages have charms and fetiches innumerable, which, in my opinion, are relics of nature-worship. The miniature house mentioned by Stanley is common to the majority of the equatorial tribes, and seems to be a kind of common fetich; *i. e.*, one that is enjoyed by the entire tribe. It is mentioned by Du Chaillu, Chaillé Long, Stanley, and many others.[25]

Du Chaillu tells of one tribe, the Bakalai, in which the women worship a particular divinity named Njambai.[26] This writer is even more inexact than Stanley, hence, we get very little scientific data from his voluminous works. From what he says of Njambai,[F] I am inclined to believe that he is a negro Priapus; this, however, is a conjectural belief and has no scientific warrant.

The Tucuña Indians of the Amazon Valley, who resemble the Passés, Jurís, and Muahés in physical appearance and customs, social and otherwise, are devil-worshipers. They are very much afraid of the *Jupari*, or devil, who seems to be "simply a mischievous imp, who is at the bottom of all those mishaps of their daily life, the causes of which are not very immediate or obvious to their dull understandings. The idea of a Creator or a beneficent God has not entered the minds of these Indians."[27]

The Peruvians, at the time of the Spanish conquest, worshiped nature; that is, the sun was deified under the name of *Pachacamac*, the Giver of Life, and was worshiped as such. The Inca, who was his earthly representative, was likewise his chief priest, though there was a great High Priest, or *Villac Vmu*, who stood at the head of the hierarchy, but who was second in dignity to the Inca.[28] The moon, wife of the sun, the stars, thunder, lightning, and other natural phenomena were also deified. But, as it invariably happens, where nature-worship is allowed to undergo its natural evolution, certain elements of phallic worship had made their appearance. These I will discuss later on.

The great temple of the sun was at Cuzco, "where, under the munificence of successive sovereigns, it had become so rich that it received the name of Coricancha, or 'the Place of Gold.'"[29] According to the *relacion* of Sarmiento, and the commentaries of Garcilasso and other Spanish writers, this building, which was surrounded by chapels and smaller edifices, and which stood in the heart of the city, must have been truly magnificent with its lavish adornments of virgin gold!

Unlike the Aztecs, a kindred race of people, the Peruvians rarely sacrificed human beings to their divinities, but, like the religion of the former, the religion of the latter had become greatly developed along ceremonial lines, as we will see later on in this essay.

It is a far cry from Peru to Japan, from the Incas to the Ainus, yet these widely separated races practiced religions that were almost identical in point of fundamental principles. Both worshiped nature, but the Peruvians were far ahead of the Ainus in civilization, and their religion, as far as ritual and ceremony are concerned, far surpassed that of the "Hairy Men" when viewed from an æsthetic standpoint. Ethically, I am inclined to believe the religion of the Ainus is just as high as was that of the Incas.

Literature is indebted to the Rev. John Batchelor for that which is, probably, the most readable book that has ever been published about these interesting people; from a scientific standpoint, however, this work is greatly lacking. Many ethnologists and anthropologists considered the Ainu autochthonic to Japan; I am forced to conclude from the evidence, however, that he is an emigrant, and that he came originally from North China or East Siberia. Be he emigrant or indigene, one thing is certain, namely, that he has been an inhabitant of the Japanese Archipelago for thousands of years. The oldest book in the Japanese language has this in it anent the Ainus: "When our august ancestors descended from heaven in a boat, they found upon this island several barbarous races, the most fierce of whom were the Ainu."[G]

The Ainu is probably the purest type of primitive man in existence. I had been led to believe by the work of Miss Bird[30] that these people were on a par with the Australians, and that they had no religious ideas whatever. (Vogt seems to advance this conclusion also,[31] while De Quatrefages[32][H] appears to have omitted this people from his tabulation. Peschel places them among the Giliaks on the Lower Amoor, and the inhabitants of the Kurile Islands.[33] These tribes are mixed nature, devil, and phallic worshipers.) Batchelor, however, shows very clearly that these people *do* have a religion, and that this religion is highly developed.

Their chief god, or rather goddess (for the Ainus regard the female as being higher than the male as far as gods are concerned), is the sun.[34] Like the Peruvians, they regard the sun as the Creator, but they are unlike them in the fact that they think that they cannot reach the goddess by direct appeal. She must be addressed through intermediaries or messengers. These messengers, the goddess of the fire, the goddess of the water, etc., are in turn addressed through the agency of *inao*, or prayer-sticks. This intermediary idea is curiously like some practices of the Roman Catholic church, or, rather, of communicants, who get the saints to carry their petitions to God.

The inao are peculiar, inasmuch as nothing exactly like them is known. The feather prayer-plumes of some of the Western Indians are used for like purposes, but these are offered directly to the Great Spirit, and not to intermediaries. "Inao, briefly described, are pieces of whittled willow wood, having the shavings attached to the top."[35] Like the Aleutians, when these people kill a bear or other wild animal, they propitiate its spirit by bestowing upon it the most fulsome compliments, and, like the religion of these Indians, the religion of the Ainus has developed along natural lines, and shows certain phallic elements.

We see from the examples here given, that religious feeling had its origin in the idea of propitiation; in fact, that it was born in fear, and by fear was it fostered. We see, furthermore, that man was not created with religious feeling as a psychical trait, but that he acquired it later on. We see, finally, that religious feeling is based, primarily and fundamentally, on one of the chief laws of nature—self-protection. The evolution and growth of Ethics demonstrate this beyond peradventure.

It is not at all probable that man in the beginning, just after his evolution from his ape-like ancestor, had, at first, any belief whatever in supernatural agencies. In his struggle for existence, all of his powers were directed toward the procurement of his food and the preservation of life; the pithecoid man was only a degree higher than the beasts in the scale of animal life. His psychic being, as yet, remained, as it were, *in ovo*, and a long period of time must have elapsed before he began to formulate and to recognize a system of theogony. After years of experience, during which the laws of heredity and progressive evolution played prominent parts, he took precedence over other animals, and his struggle for existence became easier. He then had time to study the wonderful and, to him, mysterious phenomena of nature. His limited knowledge could not explain the various natural operations by which he was surrounded, therefore he looked upon them as being mysterious and supernatural. His psychical being became active and inquiring, to satisfy which he created a system of gods which was founded on natural phenomena. At first, the gods of primitive man were, probably, few in number, and the chief god of all was the sun. Man early recognized the sun's importance in the economy of nature; this beautiful star, rising in the east in the morning, marching through the heavens during the day, and sinking behind the western horizon in the evening, must have been, to the awakening soul of man, a source of endless conjecture and debate. What was more natural than his making the sun the greatest god in his system of theogony? Man recognized in him the source of all life, and, when he arrived at an age when he could use abstract ideation in formulating his religion, he deified the life-giving function as he noticed it in himself; he began to worship the generative principle. Solar worship and its direct descendant, phallic worship, at one time or another were the religions of almost every race on the face of the globe. Solar worship, owing to its material quality, has long since been abandoned by civilized man; but phallic worship, the first *abstract* religion evolved by man, has taken deeper root; its fundamental principles are still present, though they have their seat in our subliminal consciousness, and we are, therefore, not actively conscious of their existence. But before entering on the discussion of this last point, let us turn for a time to a study of phallic worship.

CHAPTER II.
PHALLIC WORSHIP.

Phallic worship, in some form or other, has been practiced by almost every race under the sun. Indeed, among primitive peoples, those who do not practice this cult are so few in number that they have, practically, no weight whatever in a discussion of this subject. Moreover, those primitive peoples who do not worship the generative principle, either directly or indirectly, are without any religion whatsoever, and are the very lowest of all mankind in point of intelligence. I have only to cite the Tierra del Fuegians, the Bushmen, the Australians, and the Akka or Ticki-Ticki, the Pygmies of Central Africa, to prove the truthfulness of this assertion. There are other peoples who would serve as examples, but it would be a work of supererogation to enumerate them to even the casual reader.

D'Hancarville, in his magnificent work, has traced the progress of the worship of the generative principle over the entire world, while Knight, in his scholarly essay,[36] has brought out its psychological truths in a manner which cannot be surpassed. It is not my purpose to enter into a detailed account of this cult; I propose rather to discuss its probable origin in the beginning, and to give a brief outline of its history, as it is to be observed among living peoples. I wish to show, also, its connection with certain religious ceremonies and festivals of Christian peoples, which had their origin, *ab initio*, in the worship of Priapus. And, before beginning the discussion of this subject, I beg to remind the reader that a priest of Priapus regarded his sistrum as being just as sacred as a Catholic priest now considers any vessel or robe used in the service of mass, and that the priests of Brahma look on the Lingam with as much reverence and awe as did the Levites on the Ark of the Covenant and the Holy of Holies. Phallic worship is a religion, the oldest *abstract* religion in existence. Fundamentally the Creator—the Life Giver—is the phallic worshiper's god. Is he very far wrong in all that is absolutely essential? "Men think they know because they are sure they feel, and are firmly convinced because strongly agitated. Hence proceed that haste and violence with which devout persons of all religions condemn the rites and doctrines of others, and the furious zeal and bigotry with which they maintain their own, while, perhaps, if both were equally understood, both would be found to have the same meaning, and only to differ in the modes of conveying it."[37]

The Pueblo Indians of New Mexico are worshipers of the generative principle, and, like most religious sects, have evolved some very curious rites and ceremonies. The ancient temples of Venus or Aphrodite were filled with *hetarae*, who were necessary adjuncts for the proper performance of the mysteries of Priapus. These Indians, however, will not allow women to enter into their sacred ceremonies, but, on the contrary, emasculate men (by occasioning organic and functional degeneration of the sexual organs), who serve as hetaræ to the chiefs and shamans or priests.[I] These androgynes are called *mujerados*, a term which aptly describes their sexual condition.

"In order to cultivate a mujerado, a very powerful man is chosen, and he is made to masturbate excessively and ride constantly. Gradually such irritable weakness of the genital organs is engendered that, in riding, great loss of semen is induced. This condition of irritability passes into paralytic impotence. Then the testicles and penis atrophy, the hair of the beard falls out, the voice loses its depth and compass, and physical strength and energy decrease. Inclinations and disposition become feminine. The mujerado loses his position in society as a man. He takes on feminine manners and customs, and associates with women; yet, for religious reasons, he is held in high honor."[38] The phallic ceremonies of the Pueblos take place in the spring, when the life principle is exceedingly active throughout all nature.

In all probability the "botes" of the Montana Indians and the "burdachs" of the Washington tribes serve as masculine hetaræ to the chiefs and medicine men, though this has not been definitely determined. Dr. Holder described a typical "bote" of the Absaroke tribe in the New York Medical Journal, 1889. This androgyne, in many respects, resembled the mujerados of the Pueblo Indians, and probably served a like purpose in his tribe.

According to Ross, a Konyaga woman, when she has a good-looking boy, dresses him in girl's clothes and brings him up as a female. When he arrives at a suitable age he is sent to wait on the priests of the tribe and is introduced by them into the sacred mysteries of their cult; in fact, he becomes a masculine hetara.

When we read of such things we feel pretty much as Herodotus felt when he saw the naked women of Mendes submitting themselves openly ες επιδειξιν ανθρωπων to the embraces of the sacred goat.[J] To the Greek historian this act was simply horrible (τερας); and yet these Egyptians experienced no repugnance whatever. To them it represented the incarnation of the deity, and was, therefore, a sacred and holy action, just as masculine hetarism is regarded as a holy profession among the Konyagas. Phallic hetarism is one of the sacraments of the Konyaga church, and, as such, it is held in all that reverence and awe with which the savage devotee endows the mysteries of his faith.[K]

The ancient Hebrews, ancestors of one of the most ancient of the civilized races of the earth, held it in high honor. Even wise King Solomon, in the days of his old age, turned from the abstractedly pure religion of his father "to Astoreth, the goddess of the Zidonians, and to Milcom, the abomination of the Ammonites."[39] He was guilty of constructing a "high place" for Chemosh, "the abomination of Moab."[40] Any good modern biblical encyclopedia will tell the reader about Astoreth and her worship, and what the "high places" and the "groves" were.

Even the "good kings," such as Asa, Amaziah, *et al.*, did not remove the high places and the groves, for we read that, notwithstanding the fact that these kings did that which was right in the sight of the Lord, they did not remove the high places. In the case of Amaziah, it is written:

"And he did that which was right in the sight of the Lord, yet not like David, his father; he did according to all things as Joash, his father, did.

"Howbeit, the high places were not taken away: as yet the people did sacrifice and burnt incense on the high places."[41] All of the so-called "wicked kings" were phallic worshipers, and both male and female hetarism flourished during their reigns. We read of Josiah, a "good king," "And he broke down the houses of the sodomites (*kedescheim*) that were by the house of the Lord."[42] Here, in unmistakable terms (*kedescheim*), the phallic act of the hetara is specified.

Herodotus wrote: "Almost all mankind consort with women in their sacred temples, except in Greece and Egypt."[43] This is a queer mistake for a Greek to make, yet this historian is noted for his unreliability, and we should not feel surprised at this gross error. Concerning the Aphrodite of Abydos, what she was and what took place in her temples, is a matter of history. Indeed, this goddess was surnamed *Porne*! In Corinth, delubral hetarism was openly practiced; also at Bubastis and Naucratis in Egypt. Royal princesses were pallacides in the temple of Ammon; in fact, they took pride in the title of *pallakis*![L] "It is known what excessive debauchery took place in the 'groves' and 'high places' of the 'Great Goddess.' The custom was so deeply rooted that in the grotto of Bethlehem what was done formerly in the name of Adonis is to-day in the name of the Virgin Mary by Christian pilgrims; and the Mussulman *hadjis* do likewise in the sanctuaries of Mecca!"[44][M]

But let us return to primitive peoples, from whose customs and beliefs we can learn what our own ancestors must have believed before the besom of civilization swept aside the crudities of savagery.

The Khonds of India are phallic worshipers, and, in the practice of their religion, Priapus saves many a girl who would be, otherwise, offered up on the bloody altars of their divinities. The pregnant woman is sacred, hence, religious prostitution is exceedingly prevalent. But it frequently happens that some unfortunate creature, who is not pleasing to the shamans, is seized, tied to the stake and butchered.[45] As the blood flows down and deluges the ground, "the divine spirit enters into the priest and inspires him."[46] This sacrifice is of itself a phallic rite; the blood-offering is supposed to be exceedingly acceptable to Earth, the mother of all things. Blood is the essence of the life-giving principle; hence, the essence is returned to the great Giver, as a propitiatory offering.[N]

In point of fact, the worship of the generative principle is everywhere prevalent in India.[O] In the Lingam, or holy altar of the Brahmins, we see a conjunction of the male and female sexual organs, while religious prostitution, in the shape of hetarism, crowds the inner courts and corridors of almost every temple in the land with hierodules and bayaderes. The Vedas abound in references, either direct or indirect, to phallic worship. Indeed, according to some authorities, the Hindu Brahma is the same as the

Greek Pan,[P] "who is the creative spirit of the deity transfused through matter."[47]

Hundreds of pages have been written on snake-worship, in which a wonderful amount of metaphysical lore has been expended. Mr. Herbert Spencer devotes several pages to the snake, and the reason for its appearance in the religion of primitive peoples. He ascribes to savages a psychical acuteness that I am by no means willing to allow them, inasmuch as he makes them give a psychical causation for their adoption of the serpent as a deity, such as no ignorant and uncultivated savage could have possibly evolved. I am inclined to believe that, like all great students and thinkers, Mr. Spencer has a hobby, and that this hobby is animism or ancestor-worship. When he gives out, as a reason for the snake's almost universal appearance in the religions of primitive peoples, that the latter consider it an animal which has assumed the returning ghost, double, or soul of an ancestor,[48] I think that he is very much in error. There are very few primitive folk, comparatively speaking, who believe in metempsychosis. In all probability, when a race, like the ancient Egyptians, for instance, had reached a high degree of civilization, they idealized many of their religious beliefs and customs; hence, the serpent probably lost its initial and simple symbolical meaning, and stood for something higher and more ethical during the reign of the great Pharaohs, and the Golden Age of the Greeks and Latins. I am positive, however, that the snake's original significance was wholly phallic in character, and that its adoption as a symbol was simple and material, as I explain elsewhere in this essay.[Q]

I am forced to this conclusion by its presence among phallic symbols in almost every race that practiced or practices a worship of the generative principles. The Pueblo Indians, whom I have mentioned elsewhere in this treatise, regard the snake symbol with reverence; the Moqui Indians have their sacred snake dance, in which they worship the reptiles, handling the most vicious and poisonous rattlesnakes with seeming impunity; the Apaches hold that every rattlesnake is an emissary of the devil;[49] "the Piutes of Nevada have a demon deity in the form of a serpent still supposed to exist in the waters of Pyramid Lake;"[50] on the wall of an ancient Aztec ruin at Palenque there is a tablet, on which there is a cross standing on the head of a serpent, and surmounted by a bird. "The cross is the symbol of the four winds; the bird and serpent the rebus of the rain-god, their ruler."[51] The Quiche god, Hurakan, was called the "Strong Serpent," and the sign of Tlaloc, the Aztec rain-god, was a golden snake.[R] All of these tribes are or were worshipers of the generative principles, though, in most of them, phallic worship has or had lost much of its original significance.[52] In Yucatan and elsewhere in South and Central America, notably among the ruins of Chichen Itza, the serpent symbol is frequently in evidence.[53] The Indians of the Tocantins in Brazil, as well as the Muras, Mundurucus and Cucamas, are mixed nature and devil worshipers;[S] as a sequence, certain phallic rites are to be observed in their religious ceremonies.

Many of the native tribes of North America perform phallic rites at puberty. James Owen Dorsey, who has made a study of the Siouan cults, writes as follows:

"Every male Dakota sixteen years old and upward is a soldier, and is formally and mysteriously enlisted into the service of the war prophet. From him he receives the implements of war, carefully constructed after models furnished from the armory of the gods, painted after a divine prescription, and charged with a missive virtue—the tonwan—of the divinities. To obtain these necessary articles the proud applicant is required for a time to abuse himself and serve him, while he goes through a series of painful and exhausting performances, which are necessary on his part to enlist favorable notice of the gods. These performances consist chiefly of vapor baths, fastings, chants, prayers, and nightly vigils. The spear and the tomahawk being prepared and consecrated, the person who is to receive them approaches the wakan man (priest), and presents a pipe to him. He asks a favor, in substance as follows: 'Pity thou me, poor and helpless, a *woman*, and confer on me the ability to perform *manly* deeds.'"[54] According to Miss Fletcher, when an Oglala girl arrives at puberty, a great feast is prepared, and favored guests invited thereto. "A prominent feature in the feast is the feeding of these privileged persons and the girl in whose honor the feast is given, with choke cherries, as the choicest rarity to be had in the winter… In the ceremony, a few of the cherries are taken in a spoon and held over the sacred smoke and then fed to the girl."[55] This is considered one of the most sacred of their feasts.

While discussing the phallic observances of the North American races, I will introduce the subject of tattooing, though it properly belongs elsewhere in this treatise.

At puberty, the Hudson Bay Eskimos invariably tattoo their boys and girls. Lucien M. Turner writing of the latter, says:

"When a girl arrives at puberty she is taken to a secluded locality by some old woman versed in the art of tattooing, and stripped of her clothing. A small quantity of half-charred lamp wick of moss is mixed with oil from the lamp. A needle is used to prick the skin, and the pasty substance is smeared over the wound. The blood mixes with it, and in a few days a dark-bluish spot is left. The operation continues four days. When the girl returns to the tent it is known that she has begun to menstruate."[56] Both Eastern and Western Inoits celebrate puberty with certain rites. It is rather difficult, however, to get them to say much about this matter, so I will not present the evidence, meager as it is, which has been gleaned from the works of various explorers. One can readily see that much of it is conjecture, therefore of little scientific value.

Not far from the Place of Gold, the magnificent temple in which the ancient Peruvians worshiped the Life Giver, was another great edifice, styled the "House of the Virgins of the Sun." This was the domicile of the pallacides or hetæræ of the Chief Priest, the Inca. "No one but the Inca and the Coya, or queen, might enter the consecrated precincts... Woe to the unhappy maiden who was detected in an intrigue! By the stern laws of the Incas she was buried alive, her lover strangled, and the town or village to which he belonged was razed to the ground and sowed with stones as if to efface every memorial of his existence. One is astonished to find so close a resemblance between the institutions of the American Indian, the ancient Roman, and the modern Catholic. Chastity and purity of life are virtues in woman that would seem to be of equal estimation with the barbarian and with the civilized—yet the ultimate destination of the inmates of these religious houses (there were hundreds of them), was materially different... Though Virgins of the Sun, they were the brides of the Inca."[57] The monarch had thousands of these hetæræ in his various palaces. When he wished to lessen the number in his seraglios, he sent some of them to their own homes, where they lived ever after respected and revered as holy beings.[58] The religion of the Peruvians had reached a high degree of development, and many of the crudities of simple phallic worship had either been entirely abandoned or so idealized that they had been lost in the mists of ritual and ceremony. For "the ritual of the Incas involved a routine of observances as complex and elaborate as ever distinguished that of any nation, whether pagan or Christian."[59]

Notwithstanding the fact that the descendants of the Incas have been under the guardianship of the priests of the Catholic church for hundreds of years, a close, careful, painstaking, and accurate observer informs me that he has repeatedly noticed unmistakable phallic rites interwoven with their Christian ceremonials and beliefs. The same can be said of a kindred race and a kindred religion. Biart, writing of the descendants of the Aztecs, says: "In grottoes unexpectedly discovered, I have frequently found myself in the presence of Mictlanteuctli, at the foot of which a recent offering of food had been placed."[60] How exceedingly basic and fundamental the worship of the generative principle must be in Psychos itself, is indicated by these facts!

In the very beginnings of history we find that many races of people held the worship of the generative principle in high honor. Not only has the knowledge of this fact come to us through the sculptured monuments of the Egyptians and the tablets, cylinders, etc., of the Chaldeans, but it has also been set before us by ancient historians. Speaking of the Chaldeans Herodotus (1,199)[T] says, "Every woman born in the country must enter once during her lifetime the inclosure of the temple of Aphrodite, must there sit down and unite herself to a stranger. Many who are wealthy are too proud to mix with the rest, and repair thither in closed chariots, followed by a considerable train of slaves. The greater number seat themselves on the sacred pavement, with a cord twisted about their heads—and there is always a crowd there, coming and going; the women being divided by ropes into long lanes, down which strangers pass to make their choice. A woman who has once taken her place here cannot return home until a stranger has thrown into her lap a silver coin, and has led her away with him beyond the limits of the sacred inclosure. As he throws the money he pronounces these words: 'May the goddess Mylitta make thee happy!' Now among the Assyrians, Aphrodite" (*the goddess of love, desire*) "is called Mylitta. The woman follows the first man who throws her the money, and repels no one. When once she has accompanied him, and *has thereby satisfied the goddess*, she returns to her home, and from thenceforth, however large the sum offered to her, she will yield to no one." Maspero declares that "this custom still existed in the fifth century before our era, and the Greeks who visited Babylon about that time found it still in force."[61]

He also calls attention to the fact that "we meet with a direct allusion to this same custom in the Bible, in the *Book of Baruch*: The women, also, with cords about them, sitting in the ways, burn bran for perfume; but if any of them, drawn by some that passeth by, lie with him, she reproacheth her fellow, that she was not worthy of herself, nor her cord broken. Ch. VI, verse 43."

Phallic rites and observances entered very largely into the religion of the Assyrians, and can be traced back, in some form or other, even to the religion of the ancient Sumerians, the root-stock from which the Chaldeans had their origin.

In the third chapter of Hebrew history according to Moses (Genesis III), we have an unmistakable allusion to phallic worship in the use of the serpent in the myth of man's temptation and fall. The serpent was an almost universal symbol of priapic adoration throughout Egypt and Assyria; it achieved this distinction, in all probability, from its resemblance to the *instrumentum masculinum generationis*.[U] In a beautiful bronze plaque, representing Nergal, the Chaldean god of Hades, the *glans penis* of the god is distinctly the head of the snake. A splendid drawing of this plaque by Faucher-Gudin is given in Maspero's *Dawn of Civilization*.[62] It may be stated here that the uræus, or asp, which was so prominently in evidence as one of the principle signs of Egyptian royalty, was also the symbol of the life-giving principle of Ra, the sun-god.

Abraham, in all probability, instituted the rite of circumcision in remembrance of the Chaldean genital worship.[V] This sexual fetishism was eminently religious in character from its very inception among the ancient Hebrews; yet Westermarck, in his *History of Human Marriage*, considers this custom as being of ornamental origin.[63] Now, it is known beyond question of doubt that the Hebrews and Abyssinians, who practiced this rite, covered their nakedness, hence, it is folly to suppose that they ornamented a portion of their bodies which always remained carefully hidden. Moreover, since it has been in use from very ancient times "among most of the tribes inhabiting the African West Coast, among all the Mohammedan peoples, among the Kaffirs, among nearly all the peoples of Eastern Africa, among the Christian Abyssinians, Bogos, and Copts, throughout all the various tribes inhabiting Madagascar, and, in the heart of the Black Continent, among the Monbuttu and Akka; and since it is practiced very commonly in Australia, in many islands of Melanesia, in Polynesia, universally, in some parts of America, in Yucatan, on the Orinoco, and among certain tribes in Rio Branco in Brazil;"[64] and since most of these people wholly or partially hide their nakedness, it cannot, necessarily, have had its origin in the desire for ornamentation. Again, since the rite of circumcision among these peoples always takes place at puberty, when *vita sexualis* begins, and is always accompanied by other rites and ceremonies of deeply religious significance, it must be a religious observance and phallic in its nature. Girls, also, at puberty, among many tribes of Africa, among certain races of the Malayan Archipelago and South America have an operation performed upon them. "*Sunt autem gentes, quarum contrarius mos est, ut clitoris et labia minora non exsecentur, verum extendantur, et saepe longissime extendantur.*"[65] Surely such a peculiar and uncalled-for performance has a deeper significance than mere ornamentation, and does not warrant the expression "*atque ista etiam deformatio insigne pulchritudinis existimatur.*"

Tattooing, among certain races, is a phallic rite, and in the Tahitians the priapic origin of this procedure has been preserved in an interesting myth. Hinæreeremonoi was the daughter of the god and goddess Taaroa and Apouvaru. "As she grew up, in order to preserve her chasity, she was made *pahio*, or kept in a kind of inclosure, and constantly attended by her mother. Intent on her seduction, her brothers invented tattooing, and marked each other with the figure called Taomaro. Thus ornamented, they appeared before their sister, who admired the figures, and, in order to be tattooed herself, eluding the care of her mother, broke the inclosure that had been erected for her preservation, was tattooed, and became, also, the victim to the designs of her brothers. Tattooing thus originated among the gods, and was first practiced by the children of Taaroa, their principle deity. *In imitation of their example, and for the accomplishment of the same purposes it was practiced among men.*"[W][66]

With very few exceptions, primitive peoples, wherever found, have given or still give unmistakable evidence of a knowledge of phallic worship in some form or other. Many of them still practice it, generally combined with the religion from which it was evolved, *i. e.*, sun worship. The Ainu of Japan is a notable example of a race whose religion shows the presence of the elements of both worships. The religion of this remarkable people, notwithstanding the fact that it has become decidedly ethical (they having arrived at a knowledge of the good and evil principles), shows its sun birth. [X] Until very recently the *couvade* existed in full force and vigor. "As soon as a child was born, the father had to consider himself very ill, and had, therefore, to stay at home, wrapped up, by the fire. But the wife, poor creature! had to stir about as much and as quickly as possible. The idea seems to have been that *life was passing from the father into his child*."[67]

Among Slavonic races in early times, the worship of the generative principle was almost universal. This continued, in a measure, even after the establishment of Christianity, and we find phallic rites masquerading in the garb of Christian observances as late as the sixteenth century in parts of Russia and Hungary. Westermarck, in his chapter on the human rut season in primitive times, says: "Writers of the sixteenth century speak of the existence of certain festivals in Russia, at which great license prevailed. According to Pamphil, these annual gatherings took place, as a rule, at the end of June, the day before the festival of St. John the Baptist, which in pagan times was that of a divinity known by the name of Jarilo, corresponding to the Priapus of the Greeks."[68] If my memory serves me correctly, Wappäus says that a like festival was in existence among the Hungarians two hundred years ago.[69] To this day certain religious sects of Russia and Hungary are in the habit of holding orgies at which all the ceremonies of the ancient Liberalia, Floralia, and Saturnalia are duplicated. These devotees claim that, when they have reached the acme of religious enthusiasm, the spirit of God directs them, hence their licentious and lustful acts cannot be immoral.

When Great Britain was invaded and conquered by northern savages, the latter, unquestionably, introduced their own religious beliefs, which were largely phallic in character. The Teutonic god Fréa was the same as the Latin Priapus; while Friga, from whom our Friday gets its name, because this day was sacred to her, was the Teutonic Venus. Fréa is called Freyr in old Norse, and in old German, Fro.

Among the Swedes he was worshiped under the name of Fricco, and a statue of him at Upsala represented him in the characteristic attitude of the god of procreation. *"Tertius est Fricco, pacem voluptatemque largiens mortalibus, cujus etiam simulachrum fingunt ingenti priapo."*[70] From this god a vulgar word for copulation had its origin. This word is in use to-day among the descendants of the Anglo-Saxons, thus proving that the worship of the generative principle was in vogue among our own immediate ancestors.

Statuettes of Priapus, bronzes representing the sexual organs, and pottery covered with phallic scenes have been found all over England. These relics are remembrances of the Roman occupation when the worship of Priapus prevailed. In the parish of Adel, Yorkshire, was found an altar erected to Priapus, who seems to be called in this instance Mentula. At this place were found many other priapic relics, such as lamps, bracelets, amulets, etc., etc.[71] Several images of the triple phallus, as well as the single phallus, have been brought to light in London; also phallic lamps, bracelets, etc.

All over England the Anglo-Saxon Fréa, or Friga, has left remembrances of his or her worship in place-names. Fridaythorpe in Yorkshire, and Friston (Fréa's stone), which occurs in several parts of England, are examples. "We seem justified in supposing that this and other names commencing with the syllable Fri or Fry, are so many monuments of the existence of phallic worship among our Anglo-Saxon forefathers."[72] There are other words in the English language which point directly to this ancient religion; for instance, *fascinate* and *fascination*. These words were derivede directly from the Latin word *fascinum*, which was one of the names of the male organ of generation. The fascinum was worn suspended from the necks of women, and was supposed to possess magical powers; hence, to *fascinate*. Horace makes use of the word in Priapeia:

> *"Placet, Priape? Qui sunt arboris coma*
> *Sotes, sacrum revinct pampino caput,*
> *Ruber sedere cum rubente fascino."*[73]

That the worship of the fascinum was in vogue during the eighth century[Y] in Italy and in other countries under the religious jurisdiction of the Pope, the following from the *Judicia Sacerdotalia Criminibus*, clearly indicates: "If any one has performed incantation to the *fascinum*, or any incantation whatever, except one who chaunts the Creed or the Lord's Prayer, let him do penance on bread and water during three Lents."[74][Z]

During the ninth century the Council of Chalons promulgated a similar law, and in the twelfth century Buchardus repeats it, thus showing that the worship of the generative principle was continuous throughout that time.[75] That the worship of the fascinum was in vogue as late as 1247 is proven by the statutes of the Synod of Mans, which declare that he who worships the fascinum shall be seriously dealt with.[76]

In Scotland, as late as 1268, according to the Chronicles of Lanercroft, the people were in the habit of rubbing two pieces of wood together until fire was produced. At the same time an image of the phallus was elevated, and certain prayers were said to Priapus. This was the famous "need fire," and was obtained in this way in order that it might have the power of saving the cattle from the plague. Need fire was produced in this manner in the Highlands as late as 1356, at which time a cattle plague ravaged the country side. In Inverkeithing, a Catholic priest gathered all the young girls of the village and made them dance around a statue of Priapus. He himself led the dance, carrying a large wooden image of the phallus, and excited these medieval bacchantes to licentious movements and actions by his own actions and language.

When called to account by his bishop, he excused his action by stating that such performances were common in his parish. These phallic observances occurred in Easter week, March 29-April 15, 1282.[77]

In Ireland, the female sexual organs seem to have been the symbol of phallic worship most in use. In the arches over the doorways of churches, a female figure, with the person fully exposed, was invariably so placed that the external organs of generation at once caught the eye. These figures were called *Shela-na-gig*, which in Irish means "Julian the giddy." Sometimes these images were placed on the walls and used as caryatides. From this symbol the horseshoe's power to ward off evil and bring good luck has been evolved. The people in olden times were in the habit of painting, or sketching with charcoal, drawings of the female genitalia over the doors of their houses to ward off bad luck. These drawings were necessarily rude, and probably resembled a horseshoe more than they did the object for which they were intended. In course of time, when the symbol had lost its original significance, the horseshoe entirely took the place of the phallic image.

Herodotus says that Sesostris, king of Egypt, was in the habit of erecting pillars in the countries conquered by his armies, on which he had the female genitals engraved in order to show his contempt.[78] I think that the historian misinterprets the meaning of the pillars; the Egyptians were phallic worshipers, and these obelisks were, in all probability, altars to Priapus.

The beneficent influence of this particular phallic symbol has been well brought out in several classical stories. When Ceres was wandering over the world in her search after Proserpine, she came to the house of a peasant woman, Baubo by name. Baubo saw that the goddess was heart-sick and miserable, so she offered her a drink of cyceon (κυκεων). The goddess refused the refreshing mixture, and continued her lamentations. Fully believing in the virtue and efficacy of the symbol, Baubo lifted her robe and showed Ceres her genitals.[AA] The goddess burst into laughter and at once drank the cyceon.[79] The same superstition appears in a celebrated book of the sixteenth century, *Le Moyen de Parvenir*. The author of the "Worship of the Generative Powers" gives the following instructive extract from this work:

Hermès. On nomme ainsi ceux qui n'ont point vu le con de leur femme ou de leur garce. Le pauvre valet de chez nous n'étoit donc pas coquebin; il eut beau le voir.

Varro. Quand?

Hermès. Attendez, étant en fiançailles, il vouloit prendre le cas de sa fiancée; elle ne le vouloit pas: il faisoit le malade, et elle lui demandoit: "Qu'y a-t-il, mon ami?" "Hélas, ma mie, je suis si malade, que je n'en puis plus; je mourrai si je ne vois ton cas." "Vraiment voire?" dit-elle. "Hélas! oui, si je l'avois vu, je guérirois." Elle ne lui voulut point montrer; à la fin, ils furent mariés. Il advint, trois ou quatre mois après, qu'il fut fort malade; et il envoya sa femme au médicin pour porter de son eau. En allant, elle s'avisa de ce qu'il lui avoit dit en fiançailles. Elle retourna vitement, et se vint mettre sur le lit; puis, levant cotte et chemise lui présenta son cela en belle vue, et lui disoit: "Jean, regarde le con, et te guéris."[80]

Sir William Hamilton writes to Richard Payne Knight from Naples in the year 1781, as follows:

"Having last year made a curious discovery, that in a province of this kingdom, not fifty miles from its capital, a sort of devotion is still paid to Priapus, the obscene divinity of the ancients (though under another denomination), I have thought it a circumstance worth recording; particularly as it offers a fresh proof of the similitude of the Popish and Pagan religion, so well observed by Dr. Middleton in his celebrated Letter from Rome; therefore I mean to deposit the authentic proofs of this assertion in the British Museum when a proper opportunity shall offer." Sir William goes on to relate how he found many phallic amulets, charms, etc., in the possession of the people, and then describes the votive offerings laid upon the altar at a feast given in honor of Saints Cosmus and Damianus, in a church called by their names. The offerings were waxen images of the phallus. "The vows are chiefly presented by the female sex," continues he, "and they are seldom such as represent legs, arms, etc., but most commonly the male parts of generation. A person who was at this fête in the year 1780, told me that he heard a woman say, at the time she presented a vow, '*Santo Cosimo benedetto, cosi lo voglio.*'"[81]

This church was in Isernia, a little village about fifty miles from Naples, and away from the direct line of travel, hence its inhabitants saw little of the world, and therefore kept to their old customs longer than their more favored neighbors. Thus it happened that, even in the latter half of the eighteenth century, Priapus had his votaries almost within the shadow of the Vatican! These phallic rites were finally abolished by episcopal command.

One of the most common amulets or charms against *jettitura*, or the "evil eye," the *bête noire* of every Italian, is a little coral hand. The middle finger of this hand is extended, thus representing the penis, while the other fingers are closed on the palm, thus representing the testicles. In ancient times, when a man extended his hand, closed in this manner, it was a gesture of insult and anger; to-day this gesture is only made in derision and contempt. The hand closed in this way, or, rather, with the thumb projecting between the first and second fingers (another very common phallic symbol or sign), was called a "fig"; hence, the old expression of contempt and indifference, "a fico for you, sir," now modernized into "I don't care a fig."[AB]

France, as well as Italy, had her phallic charms and her phallic saints. Priapus was a god to the ancients—to the people of the Middle Ages he was a saint. According to M. Dulaure, in the south of France, Provence, Languedoc, and the Lyonnais, he was worshiped under the name of St. Foutin. This name is derived from that of the first bishop of Lyons, Fotinus, to whom the people had transferred (as they have done to many other sainted individuals) the distinguishing characteristics of a god; in this instance, Priapus. At Lyons there was an immense wooden phallus, and the women were in the habit of scraping this image, and then steeping the wood-dust in water, which they drank as a remedy against barrenness. Sometimes they gave it to the men in order to stimulate sexuality or sensuality. At Varailles, in Provence, waxen images of the male and female sexual organs were offered to St. Foutin, and, since these images were suspended from the ceiling and moved by every vagrant current of air, the effect was sometimes very astonishing. *"Témoin Saint Foutin de Varailles en Provence, auquel sont dédiées les parties honteuses de l'un et de l' autre sexe, formées en cire; le plancher de la chapelle en est fort garni, et, quand le vent les fait entrebattre, cela débauche un peu les dévotions à l'honneur de ce Saint."*[82]

This worship at Varailles was identical with that of Isernia; the votive offerings were waxen images or models of the genital organs, while the saints differed only in name, not in character. At Embrun the worship of St. Foutin was a little different. The women at this last mentioned place poured wine on the phallus; this wine was collected in a bucket, and, when it became sour, it was used as a medicine for barrenness.

When Embrun was besieged and taken by the Protestants in 1585, this phallus was found among the other sacred relics, and its head "was red with the wine which had been poured upon it."[83] In the church of St. Eutropius, at Orange, a large phallus covered with leather was seized and burnt by the Protestants in 1562. Dulaure says that the sexual organs were objects of worship at Porighy, Viviers, Vendre in the Bourbonnais, Cives, Auxerre, Puy-en-Velay, and at hundreds of other places. Some of these phalli were recreated as fast as they were worn away by zealous devotees. They were so arranged in the walls of the churches that, "as the phallic end in front became shortened (by scrapings), a blow from a mallet from behind thrust it forward, so that it was restored to its original length."[84]

In the public square of Batavia there was formerly kept a bronze cannon which had been captured from the natives. The touch-hole of this piece of ordnance was made in the shape of a phallic hand or "fig," which I have described elsewhere. The barren Malay women were in the habit of seating themselves on this hand in order that they might become pregnant.[AC] An analogous custom was prevalent in France and elsewhere in Europe during the Middle Ages. This habit led to sexual abuses, and was finally condemned by the ecclesiastical authorities. Indeed, the Church inflicted severe penances on the women who were guilty of using phalli: "*Mulier qualique molimine aut se ipsam aut cum altera fornicans tres annos poeniteat, unum ex his pane et aqua. Cum sanctimoniali per machinam fornicans, annos septem poeniteat, duos ex his in pane et aqua.*"[85] We see by this that nuns were more severely punished than were other women.

This use of the phallus is mentioned in the Bible, where it is bitterly condemned by one of the prophets: "Thou hast also taken thy fair jewels of my gold and of my silver, which I had given thee, and madest to thyself images of men, and didst commit whoredom with them."[86] Finally, it was the custom of the young girls of France during the Middle Ages (like the maidens of certain savage races), who were on the eve of marriage, to offer up to St. Foutin their last maiden robes. From the evidence here adduced, we see that phallic worship existed in some parts of Europe as late as the latter half of the eighteenth century, and that it was almost universal during the Middle Ages. According to Becan,[87] Golnitz,[88] and other historians, there were several other phallic saints besides St. Foutin who were worshiped in Belgium, Spain, Germany and other European countries; but, since their adoration was similar to that of St. Foutin, I do not think it necessary to give a description of it here. It has been shown conclusively that worship of the generative principle was in vogue among the Latins, the Greeks, the ancient Germans, the Saxons, the Danes, the Gauls, the Iberians, the Picts, the Celts and the Britons. It has been demonstrated, also, that vestiges of phallic worship existed in England, France, Italy, Spain and Germany during the Middle Ages. As late as the latter part of the eighteenth century wax images of the phallus were used as votive offerings in the town of Isernia, not many miles from Naples; the beribboned Maypole of our Mayday festival is but the flower decked phallus of the Roman matrons; charms against *jettitura*, "the evil eye," little coral hands with the middle finger extended (in ancient days one of the most common symbols of Priapus) can still be purchased in the streets of Rome.[AD] "This worship" (that of Priapus) "which was but part of that of the generative powers, appears to have been the most ancient of the superstitions of the human race, and has prevailed more or less among all known peoples before the introduction of Christianity; and, singularly enough, *so deeply it seems to have been implanted in human nature* that even the promulgation of the gospel did not abolish it, for it continued to exist, accepted and often encouraged by the medieval clergy."[89]

So very ancient was the inception of the worship of the generative principle that we have some reason for believing that even the cave-dwellers practiced this cult. It was stated in the *Moniteur*, January, 1865, that "in the province of Venice, in Italy, excavations in a bone-cave have brought to light, beneath ten feet of stalagmite, bones of animals, mostly post-tertiary, of the usual description found in such places, flint implements, with a needle of bone having an eye and point, and a plate of argillaceous compound, on which was scratched a rude drawing of the phallus."[90] Thus we see that, possibly, from the time of the cave-dwellers to almost the beginning of the nineteenth century, phallic worship existed in Southern Europe! From the Sagas, folklore tales, and myths of the Norse we have every reason for believing that it existed for almost as great a length of time in Northern Europe. That in Western Europe, before and during the Middle Ages, it flourished in a variety of forms, we have unimpeachable testimony.

In this brief outline of phallic worship I have endeavored to show that the worship of the generative principle has been universal; that it is still practiced by primitive peoples, and that vestiges of it lingered among certain civilized peoples until, comparatively speaking, a recent time. In order to show what a height of idealization and abstraction it had reached at a time when Greece stood at the head of the civilized world, I will close this part of my essay with the following quotation from Knight's strong, erudite, and exhaustive treatise: "The ancient theologists ... finding that they could conceive no idea of infinity, were content to revere the Infinite Being in the most general and efficient exertion of his power—attraction; whose agency is perceptible through all matter, and to which all motion may, perhaps, be ultimately traced. His agency being supposed to extend through the whole material world, and to produce all the various revolutions by which its system is sustained, his attributes were, of course, extremely numerous and varied. These were expressed by various titles and epithets in the mystic hymns and litanies, which the artists endeavored to represent by various forms and characters of men and animals. The great characteristic attribute was represented by the organ of generation in that state of tension and rigidity which is necessary to the due performance of its functions. Many small images of this kind have been found among the ruins of Herculaneum and Pompeii, attached to bracelets, which the chaste and pious matrons of antiquity wore round their necks and arms. In these the organ of generation appears alone, or accompanied by the wings of incubation, in order to show that the wearer devoted herself wholly and solely to procreation, the great end for which she was ordained. So expressive a symbol, being constantly in view, must keep her attention fixed on its natural object, and continually remind her of the gratitude she owed the Creator for having taken her into his service, made her partaker of his most valuable blessings, and employed her as the passive instrument in the exertion of his most beneficial power. The female organs of generation were revered as symbols of the generative power of nature or matter, as the male's were of the generative powers of God."[91]

CHAPTER III.
THE PSYCHICAL CORRELATION OF RELIGIOUS EMOTION AND SEXUAL DESIRE.

That there exists a relationship between the cultivated ethical emotion, religious feeling, and the essentially natural physio-psychical function, sexual desire or *libido*, is a fact noticed and commented on by many thinkers and writers. The literature of the subject is, however, exceedingly fragmentary and disconnected, no author (as far as I have been able to determine) having devoted as much as one thousand words to the consideration of this very interesting psychical phenomenon. Hence, my data have been gathered from many sources, which are as diversified as they are numerous.

Beyond a question of doubt, man becomes religiously enthused most frequently either early in life, when pubescence is, or is about to be, established, or late in life, when sexual desire has become either entirely extinct or very much abated. Young boys and girls are exceedingly impressionable at, or just before, puberty, and are apt to embrace religion with the utmost enthusiasm. A distinguished evangelist declares that "men and women seldom or never enter into the kingdom of God after they have arrived at maturity. Out of a thousand converts, seven hundred are converted before they are twenty years old."[92]

The Roman Catholic church is keenly alive to these facts, therefore requires the rite of confirmation to be administered, if possible, to its would-be communicants at, or before, the age of puberty.[AE]

Of all the insanities of the pubescent state, erotomania and religious mania are the most frequent and the most pronounced. Sometimes they go hand in hand, the most inordinate sensuality being coupled with abnormal religious zeal. A young woman of my acquaintance, whose conduct has given rise to much scandal, is, at times, a reincarnate Messalina, while at other times she is the very embodiment of ethical and religious purity. Another young girl, in whom *vita sexualis* was about to be established, became religiously insane and had delusions in which she declared that she was in heaven and sitting at the right hand of God. She declared this over and over again, while shamelessly committing manustrupation! Krafft-Ebing calls attention to this relation between religious and sexual feeling in psycho-pathological states. "It suffices," says he, "to recall how intense sensuality makes itself manifest in the clinical history of many religious maniacs; the motley mixture of religious and sexual delusions that is so frequently observed in psychoses (*e. g.*, in maniacal women who think they are or will be the mother of God), but particularly in masturbatic insanity; and finally, the sexual, cruel self-punishment, injuries, self-castrations, and even self-crucifixions, resulting from abnormal religio-sexual feeling."[93]

An example of the last mentioned self-immolation (self-crucifixion) is given by Berghierri, and is a remarkable instance of the interchangeableness of religious emotion and sexual desire in psychopathic individuals. The man in question, who had been intensely sensual, manufactured a cross, nailed himself to it, and ingeniously managed to suspend himself and cross from the window of his sleeping apartment.

"All through the history of insanity the student has occasion to observe this close alliance of sexual and religious ideas; an alliance which may be partly accounted for because of the prominence which sexual themes have in most creeds, as illustrated in ancient times by the phallus worship of the Egyptians, the ceremonies of the Friga cultus of the Saxons, the frequent and detailed reference to sexual topics in the Koran and several other books of the kind, and which is further illustrated in the performances which, to come down to a modern period, characterize the religious revival and camp-meeting as they tinctured their medieval model, the Münster Anabaptist movement."[94]

Men, owing to their greater freedom, soon learn the difference of the sexes and the delights of sexual congress; women, hedged in by conventionalities and deterred by their innate passivity, remain, for the most part, in ignorance of sexual knowledge until their marriage. For this reason it happens that very many more women than men experience religious emotion. *Young married men and women, who are in perfect sexual health, and who have not experienced religion before marriage, seldom give this emotion a single thought until late in life, when both libido and vita sexualis are on the wane or are extinct.* Voltaire cynically, though truthfully, observes that when woman is no longer pleasing to man she then turns to God. A woman who has been disappointed in love almost invariably seeks consolation in religion. The virtuous unmarried woman, who has been unsuccessful in the pursuit of a husband, invariably turns to God and religion with impassioned zeal and energy.

Ungratified, or, rather, *unsatisfied*, sensuality very frequently gives rise to great religio-sexual enthusiasm. The circumcised foreskin of Christ, where it was and what had become of it, was a source of continual worriment to the nun Blanbekin; in an ecstacy of ungratified *libido*, St. Catherine of Genoa would frequently cast herself on the hard floor of her cell, crying: "Love! love! I can endure it no longer;" St. Armelle and St. Elizabeth were troubled with *libido* for the child Jesus;[95] an old prayer is quite significant: "Oh, that I had found thee, Holy Emanuel; *Oh, that I had thee in my bed to bring delight to body and soul!* Come and be mine, and my heart shall be thy resting-place."[96] Francis Parkman calls attention to the fact that the nuns sent over to America in colonization days were frequently seized with religio-sexual frenzy. "She heard," writes he of Marie de l'Incarnation, "in a trance, a miraculous voice. It was that of Christ, promising to become her spouse. Months and years passed, full of troubled hopes and fears, when again the voice sounded in her ear, with assurance that the promise was fulfilled, and that she was, indeed, his bride. Now ensued phenomena which are not infrequent among Roman Catholic female devotees, when unmarried, or married unhappily, and *which have their source in the necessities of a woman's nature.*" (The italics are my own.) "To her excited thought, her divine spouse became a living presence; and her language to him, as recorded by herself, is of intense passion. She went to prayer, agitated and tremulous, as if to a meeting with an earthly lover: 'Oh, my Love,' she exclaimed, 'when shall I embrace you? Have you no pity on the torments that I suffer? Alas! alas! my Love, my Beauty, my Life! Instead of healing my pain, you take pleasure in it. Come, let me embrace you, and die in your sacred arms!'"[97] The historian remarks that the "holy widow," as her biographers call her, is an example, and a lamentable one, of the tendency of the erotic principle to ally itself with high religious excitement and enthusiasm. Further along he says that "some of the pupils of Marie de l'Incarnation, also, had mystical marriages with Christ; and the impassioned rhapsodies of one of them being overheard, she nearly lost her character, as it was thought that she was apostrophizing an earthly lover."[98]

The instances of religio-sexual outbursts in nuns and Roman Catholic female devotees who lead celibate lives are very numerous; I will, however, call attention to but one other: St. Veronica was so much in love with the divine lion that she took a young lion to bed with her, fondled and kissed it, and allowed it to suck her breasts.[99] Throughout sacred literature, beginning with the Bible itself, religio-sexual feeling is very much *en evidence*. Hosea married a prostitute because—so he declared—God commanded him so to do. If Solomon's beautiful song is typical of the Church and the Christ (as some theologians teach), then it is an unmistakable instance of religio-sexual feeling; religious emotion and sexual desire walk hand in hand through the measures of this impassioned verse. Circumcision, now eminently a religious ceremony, was, unquestionably, a sexual fetich and a phallic rite, which has been handed down from antiquity, when all the world were phallic worshipers! The very pillars set up by the patriarchs in commemoration of certain events were but rude images of the phallus, while not a few of the mysteries of the Holy of Holies itself were but vestiges of Chaldean and Egyptian genital worship! [AF]

That a relationship between, and an interchangeableness of, these two widely dissimilar psychical operations, *i.e.*, religious emotion and sexual desire, does exist, there can be no doubt.[AG] Now, what is the cause of, the reason for, this relationship? Mantegazza, Maudsley, Schleiermacher, Krafft-Ebing, and many others have endeavored, incidentally, to assign reasons for this relationship, but have, in my opinion, signally failed. Spitzka has tentatively, and without elaborating his idea in the least, suggested a theory which, I believe, solves the problem in every essential point. Says he in "Insanity," page 39: This "alliance" (between religious emotion and *libido*) "may be partly accounted for because of the prominence which sexual themes have in most creeds, as illustrated in ancient times by the phallus worship of the Egyptians, the ceremonies of the Friga cultus of the Saxons, the frequent and detailed reference to sexual topics in the Koran and several other books of the kind, etc." Dr. Spitzka does not enter into any discussion of the matter; he simply asserts his belief in the cause of the relationship, and then dismisses the subject without further comment.

Now, permit me, as briefly as possible, to designate the cause of the relationship between, and the interchangeableness of, religious feeling and sexual desire, which, as I believe, is to be found in the once widespread existence of phallic worship.

Some ten or twelve years ago, in an article on Suicide, which was published in the *American Practitioner and News*, I suggested (as a possible explanation for certain psychical phenomena) the existence in man of two consciousnesses, an active, vigilant consciousness and a pseudo-dormant consciousness. Again, in the *American Naturalist*, in an essay entitled "The Psychology of Hypnotism,"[100] I reasserted this theory and, to a certain extent, elaborated it. I placed man's active consciousness in the cortical portion of the brain, and his pseudo-dormant, *unconscious* consciousness (arbitrarily, be it confessed) in the basilar ganglia, and called this latter consciousness, "ganglionic consciousness."

Recently, much has been written on the doctrine of duplex personality, notably by Mr. F. W. H. Myers, in a series of papers read before the Society of Psychical Research. Professor Newbold has also written very entertainingly and instructively on this subject. While not fully accepting the theory of "duplex personality," *i. e.*, active consciousness and *subliminal consciousness* (Myers' name for the pseudo-dormant consciousness), as having been proven, Newbold says: "Of all the theories developed from the point of independence, Mr. Myers' is the most comprehensive in its scope, is kept in most constant touch with what the author regards as facts, and displays the greatest philosophic insight."[101] According to the theory of duplex personality, many instincts, desires, and emotions have been crowded out of the active consciousness and have been relegated to the pseudo-dormant consciousness. This has been brought about by a "process of selection out of an infinity of possible elements solely on the grounds of utility." Thus the *cause* for our horror of incest is hidden away in our subliminal consciousness; yet we cannot but think, with Westermarck, that this instinct is but the result of natural selection,[102] the utility of the factor or factors occasioning it being no longer in evidence or required. Again, at certain seasons, man is seized with *waldliebe* (forest-love) and longs to flee from the haunts of men, and, with gun and rod, to revert, as far as possible, to the state of his savage ancestors. The desire is safely hidden away in his subliminal consciousness until favoring circumstances tempt it forth. It is not alone in "sleep, dreams, hypnosis, trance, and ecstacy that we see a temporary subsidence of the upper consciousness and the upheaval of a subliminal stratum"; there are many other states and many other causes for this strange psychical phenomenon.

I have demonstrated in the preceding pages that the worship of the generative principle was almost, if not wholly, universal; I have also shown that the beliefs, rites, and ceremonies of this cult made a lasting impression upon the minds of every people among whom it gained a foothold. Take the case of the ancient Hebrews. Notwithstanding the fact that they were tried in the furnace of Javeh's awful wrath time and again; notwithstanding the fact that famine, pestilence, war, and imprisonment destroyed them by thousands; and, notwithstanding the fact that they were threatened with utter and absolute annihilation—all on account of this cult—they would not wholly abandon it. The words of the prophets become almost pathetic as we read, over and over again, that, although the kings did that which was pleasing in the sight of the Lord, "the high places and the groves were not destroyed." Take the case of the Aztecs. Crushed beneath the iron heels of Spain's hardy buccaneers, an utterly broken and conquered race, Cortez turned them over to the ministering care of his zealous priests. The prison, agonizing torture, and the awful stake succeeded, at last, in Christianizing them; they became children of Holy Mother Church! And yet, hundreds of years after this "glorious victory of the cross," Biart finds the humble offerings of their descendants at the feet of Mictlanteuctli! The modern Christian Indian, in the deep shadows of the night, steals forth to offer up in secrecy a prayer at the feet of one of the phallic trinity! What matters it to the modern Aztec that his petition is offered to the ruler of Mictlan, the hell of his forefathers, instead of to the mighty Ipalnemoani, the Life-Giver?[103] In his opinion, Mictlanteuctli represents the entire Aztec theogony, for has not his white priest kept the name of *this* god green in his memory? All the other gods have been forgotten; their personalities have been absorbed into that of the god of hell, for he has had advertisers in the shape of Catholic priests ever since the fall of the Aztec Empire! Take the case of the Peruvians. Although the Place of Gold and the beautiful Virgins of the Sun are not even memories to the descendants of the Incas, the religion which gave rise to them is not wholly forgotten; "phallic rites and ceremonies are to be observed interwoven with their Christian ritual and belief!" Take the case of the Roman Catholic devotees of Isernia, of Varailles, of Lyons, of hundreds of other places during the latter half of the eighteenth century. Priapus died when the first Christian emperor took his seat on the throne of Imperial Rome, and yet, hundreds and hundreds of years thereafter, we behold some of the mysteries of Eleusis almost within the shadow of St. Peter's!

Now, why is this? There can be but one answer, and that is that these people simply inherited a portion of the *psychos* of their forefathers, which made the tenets of this religion natural and easy of belief. I have demonstrated, I believe, that religious feeling was not a psychical trait in the beginning; like a number of other mental attributes, it was the result of evolution.[104] Mental abstraction, especially as associated with religious feeling, was the result of psychical growth, of psychically inherited experiences.[AH] As *psychos* grew beneath the fostering influence of ages of experience, the mind became able to formulate abstract thought. In the beginning, the process of ratiocination was, necessarily, very simple; but, simple as it was, it was able to recognize the source of life—first, in the sun, then, in the second place, in man himself; and, finally and *abstractly*, in a source outside of, but connected with, man. This abstract source, which sprung from sexuality, *ab initio*, they deified and worshiped. Thus we see that, in the very beginning, the worship of the generative principle sprung from, and was a part of, man himself. Throughout thousands and thousands of years, religious feeling and sexual desire, the component parts of phallic adoration, were intimately associated; finally, religio-sexuality became an instinct, just as a belief in the existence of a double or soul became an instinct.

Belief in the existence of a soul has never been repressed; its utility is still recognized; hence, it is present in our active consciousness. The accumulated experiences of civilization have, however, declared the inutility of phallic worship, hence, it has been crowded out of our active consciousness by a process of selection and has been relegated to the innermost recesses of our subliminal consciousness, where also dwell many other formerly active instincts of our savage ancestors. When circumstances favoring their appearances occur, these pseudo-dormant instincts always become evident; it is due to this fact that the correlation of religious emotion and sexual desire exists.

VIRAGINITY AND EFFEMINATION.

In following up the chain of evolution in animal life from its inception in primordial protoplasm to its end, as we now find it, we discover that the interlinking organisms are, in the beginning, either asexual or hermaphroditic. The moneron, the lowest form of animal life, simply multiplies by division. The different elements through which propagation and generation are carried on, are undoubtedly present even in the moneron, but are not differentiated. The moneron is an organless, structureless organism, consequently asexual. The cell, on the contrary, is hermaphroditic, for it contains within itself the necessary elements for reproducing itself. The amœba is the connecting link which connects all terrene life with primitive bathybian protoplasm, and is, strictly speaking, a true hermaphrodite. Ascending at once to the sixth stage in the ancestry of man, we come to the *acoelomi*, or worms without body cavity. These worms are phylogenetic, consequently hermaphroditic. I do not mean to say that these worms have the organs of each sex equally developed; therefore, in the use of the word hermœphrodite, I use it in its broadest sense. I simply mean that they are autogenetic. In the *rhabdocoela* the sexual organs appear in their simplest forms—a testis anterior to a single or double ovary. Other gliding worms have a more complex arrangement of the sexual organs, but most of them are true hermaphrodites. Next in the chain of evolutionary development, and one step nearer man, we find the soft worms (*scolecidae*); from a branch of this family the parent group of vertebrates was developed. The immediate ancestor of the vertebrates was either the amphioxus (lancelet) or some other notochordate animal, whose type is now extinct. Thus we have traced hermaphroditism from the amœba to the amphioxus, from the ancestor of the parent cell to the ancestor of the vertebrates. We could carry it further, but it is unnecessary. Effemination and viraginity, are due directly to the influence of that strange law laid down by Darwin—the law of reversion to ancestral types. It is an effort of nature to return man to the old hermaphroditic form from which he was evolved. It is an effort on the part of nature to incorporate the individualities of the male and female, both physical and psychical, in one body. The phenomenon of atavism is more apt to occur in feeble types than in strong, healthy and well-developed types. Microcephalism, occurring, as it most frequently does, among ignorant, ill-nourished, and unhealthy people, is an example. Dolichocephalism and a flattening of the cranial arch, with corresponding loss of capacity in the skull—types that we see everywhere among the depraved and vicious—are other examples of this tendency of atavism to seize on weakened and unhealthy subjects. Effemination finds more victims among the wealthy and the educated than among the poor and uneducated. This phenomenon is a psychic rather than a physical hermaphroditism, and is directly traceable to the enervation produced by the habits of the wealthy and unemployed. Wealth begets luxury, luxury begets debauchery and consequent enervation. Periods of moral decadence in the life of a nation are always coincident with periods of luxury and great wealth, with consequent enervation and effemination; examples of this may be found in the histories of Rome, Greece, and France. During the reign of Louis XV., examples of effemination crowded into the court and vied with the royal fop in the splendor of their raiment and effeminacy of their bearing. Psychic hermaphroditism does not occur *naturally* in uncivilized or half-civilized races. The reason for this is patent. Atavism finds among them no weakened and enervated subjects on whom to perpetrate this strange travesty on nature.

Large cities are the hotbeds and breeding-places of the various neuroses. There general paresis treads closely upon the heels of sexual neurasthenia, while the victims of hysteria and kindred ills are almost countless in their number. What wonder, then, that the offspring of such parents should be weak and neurasthenic, and fall easy victims to the thousand and one erotic fancies which beset them! What wonder that here atavism finds its richest field, and plays its strangest and most fearful pranks, sending men into the world with the tastes, desires, and habits of women, and women with all the mental hibitudes of men! Juvenal wrote in scathing, searing sarcasm of the degeneracy of the Roman youth; effemination was very prevalent, and this bitter satirist wrote burning words against their degrading and bestial practices. It seems to me that we are beginning to need a Juvenal for this day and generation!

People divide themselves into classes, and these classes are generally exceedingly clannish. It is not considered "good form" to marry out of the class to which an individual may belong, consequently, no new types of individuals are added. Luxury and debauchery enervate the classes which indulge in them. The people of these classes intermarry among themselves, no new blood is added, hence, in a very few generations, degeneration sets in.

Effemination and viraginity are common types of degeneration which always follow in the wake of luxury and debauchery. Effemination makes its appearance early in life. The young boy likes the society of girls; he plays with dolls, and, if permitted, will don female attire and dress his hair like a girl. He learns to sew, to knit, to embroider, to do "tatting." He becomes a connoisseur in female dress, and likes to discuss matters pertaining to the toilet of females. He does not care for boyish sports, and when he grows older, takes no pleasure in the amusements and pursuits of his masculine acquaintances. He prefers to spend his time with women and to engage in their employments and amusements. As the change in his psychic being becomes more pronounced and more overpowering, he will endeavor to approach the female in gait, attitude, and style of dress.

I have seen mothers guilty of incalculable harm by fostering such inclinations in their sons. They think (the thought is a natural one) that such perversions of taste indicate gentleness and kindliness, and induce their sons to continue in the practice of them, thus assisting atavism in its baneful work.

Effemination is a disease which, taken at its inception, can generally be eradicated and cured. As soon as it is discovered, the boy's surroundings should be changed; his mind should be directed into new channels, and his dormant boy's nature aroused. Outdoor exercise and a free intercourse with companions of his own sex should be made important factors in the treatment of an incipient effeminant. He should be carefully watched until *vita sexualis* has been established; he should then be taught the dangers of youthful follies and indiscretions.

A dandified man is always ridiculous, but when he adds to his foppery, effemination, he then becomes contemptible.

Several years ago I had the opportunity of studying a pronounced effeminant. He is one of the best known young men of a Southern city, and is a leader in society. He took me to his "boudoir" and showed me his "lingerie." The words quoted are his own. His nightgowns were marvels of artistic needlework, as far as I was able to judge, and were made by himself. His nightcaps were "sweetly pretty," and one of them was a "perfect dream of beauty." On his dressing-table were all the accessories of a modern society woman's toilet, including rouge, powder, a complete manicure set, and numerous bottles of perfumes and toilet waters. In his wardrobe he had displayed on forms, some six or eight corsets and chemisettes—"corset-covers," as he designated them.

This man's voice and manner of speaking are decidedly feminine; all the little mannerisms and affectations of a society woman being faithfully reproduced. I understand from his associates that he is a splendid business man, and that not a breath of scandal has ever tarnished his good name. He was reared by his mother, and never associated with boys until his sixteenth year. I understood from him that she always treated him as a girl, and consulted him in all things pertaining to her toilet. He seemed utterly unconscious of his anomalous condition, and as his business associates are gentlemen, and his intimate friends are ladies, he may drift through life without a single jar to mar the serenity of his existence.

Viraginity is, comparatively, an infrequent occurrence, but under its influence the unfortunate victims are guilty of startling vagaries. The recent case of Alice Mitchell, who killed Miss Ward, at Memphis, Tenn., is an example of pronounced viraginity. We see daily in the newspapers accounts of women who masquerade as men, and history abounds in like instances. The celebrated writer Count Sandor V. was a woman who posed as a man, and who was in fact Sarolta (Charlotte), Countess V. "Among many foolish things that her father encouraged in her was the fact that he brought her up as a boy, called her Sandor, allowed her to ride, drive, and hunt, admiring her muscular energy." At the age of thirteen she ran away from school, where she had been sent by her mother, and returned home. "Sarolta returned to her mother, who, however, could do nothing and was compelled to allow her daughter to again become Sandor, wear male clothes, and, at least once a year, to fall in love with persons of her own sex."

Mothers, early in life, though not from any sense of danger to their daughters, begin to eradicate the tom-boy inclinations in their female children; hence the comparative infrequency of viraginity. The congenital viragint will always remain somewhat masculine in her tastes and ideas, but her inclinations and desires having been turned toward femininity early in life, she will escape the horrors of complete viraginity or gynandry. The victim of effemination, however, is saved by no such accidental forethought. The ignorant mother fosters feminine inclinations and desires in her effeminate son until his psychic being becomes entirely changed, and not even the establishment of *vita sexualis* will save him from effemination.

An only son, who is in the least degree neurasthenic, runs the risk of becoming an effeminant under the tutelage of a loving but ignorant mother who encourages his feminine tastes and inclinations. A young man of my acquaintance, who is an only son, is so situated. This young man devotes his entire attention to matters of the toilet. He paints his cheeks and powders his face; even his eyebrows and eyelashes are anointed with some dark-colored ointment or pomade.

Effemination and viraginity are more prevalent in the Old World than in the United States. The civilization and settlement of the United States are, comparatively speaking, new. The people are, as yet, a young, strong, and vigorous nation. Years of luxury and debauchery have not yet brought the penalty of enervation and neurasthenia to the *masses,* though in certain circles of society, it is becoming painfully evident that that penalty is being even now exacted.

In this article I have described only mild types of viraginity and effemination. In the more pronounced types of these singular examples of atavism or reversion, the victims commit the most unheard of and the most unnatural acts.

Almost every case of effemination or viraginity can be cured if recognized and treated in its incipiency. The parents should be the physicians. They should keep a watchful supervision over their offspring, and as soon as any evidences of effemination or viraginity become apparent, treatment, both physical and psychical, should at once be instituted.

Effemination has occasioned the downfall of many nations; let us guard against it with all our power. Let us train up our boys to be manly men, and our girls to be womanly women.

BORDERLANDS AND CRANKDOM.

When that bilious critic and merciless crucifier of human foibles, Carlyle, himself a degenerate, wrote that nine-tenths of the world were fools, he was much nearer truth than most men think. When we take an introspective view of our sane personality, we shudder to see how near it is to the borderlands of insanity and the bizarre and eccentric world of crankdom. There hardly lives a man who does not possess some eccentricity, or who does not cherish, hidden, perhaps, deep within himself, some small delusion, which he is ashamed to acknowledge to the outside world. Social relations and the iron rules of custom hold in place the balance-wheel of many a disordered mind. The mental equipoise is kept at the normal standard only by the powerful aid of the will, supported and assisted by extraneous adjuvants, such as fear of punishment, fear of personal harm, and, above all, by the fear of ridicule. Many a man hugs his delusions closely to his heart, indulges them only in the secret recesses of his soul, and, their sole owner and acquaintance, carries them with him to his grave.

Any man who has a retentive memory, and one capable of minute analysis, can look back in his life and recall moments when his insane personality got the better of his will, and ran riot in forbidden pathways. He may not have committed an insane act; yet the thought, the impulse, the delusion was there and only outside influences kept it from breaking forth. Who fails to remember certain times in his life when he has had an almost overpowering desire to cry out in church, or to laugh on some sad or solemn occasion; or, having a razor in his hand, has had an impulse, sudden and intense, to draw it across his throat; or, being on some high place, has been seized with the desire to hurl himself downward? This shows how near indeed the healthy mind ever hovers on the borderlands of insanity.

Man stands so close to the portals of insanity that he can look through the gateway, when he takes an introspective view of his psychical being, and can see the phantoms and mental ghosts of his insane personality.

We have every reason to believe that, among civilized races, there is a vast amount of latent insanity. Taking the tables of our insane asylums, we find a thousand and one causes given as the exciting factors in the mental overthrow. Love, religion, anger, disappointment, etc., down through the long list of psychic and æsthetic emotions, until it seems as though even a breath of wind would be sufficient to destroy the mental equipoise.

Among savage and uncivilized races, insanity is of infrequent occurrence. Only when a race begins to elevate itself and take on a higher view of morality, when new rules and new laws, new customs and innovations, tending to place individuals in a state of comparison, arise, does insanity make its appearance. The untutored savage, living in a state of communism, is untroubled by the jealousies and heart-burnings of his civilized congener. He lives in the to-day and allows the to-morrow to take care of itself. Devoid of ambition, a mere animal, sensual and indolent, he cares only for the gratification of his physical desires. The mental attributes of a civilized being are, in him, wanting.

Psychos is the result of evolutionary development, and the chief reason why insanity is not as prevalent in the savage as in the civilized man, is because the brain of the savage lacks development. I do not wish to convey the idea that insanity is purely psychical in its nature. Insanity is the result of a material change in the structure of the brain produced by morbific action. The manifestations of insanity are merely the symptoms of a disease that involves the brain. The savage has less development of psychical function, consequently he is less liable to mental lesion. I mean by psychical function that portion of the brain in which psychos has its origin. Alienists consider the habits of men as being the factor in the production of insanity. Habits and heredity are undoubted factors in the production of diseased minds, and, in fact, are the chief agents. You cannot, however, expect to find a disordered function where that function is absent. Savages have paresis, apoplexy, and imbecility, seldom or never insanity. The reason is patent—they lack the psychic function, that peculiar element, whatever it may be, which raises civilized man so high above them. That this element can be developed in savages I do not for one instant deny. The ploughshare of evolutionary civilization will bring it to the surface sooner or later, and when it does insanity follows. I have only to point to the American negro to prove the truth of my proposition; even he is partially exempt, simply because his civilization is of such recent date that his brain has not yet acquired its full quota of the psychic element.

I will venture to assert, so true is the fact that insanity is the product of civilization, that, if it were not for the combating influences of social laws, assisted not a little by scientific medical aid, all North America could not contain the vast and enormous army that would constitute the civilized world's array of lunatics.

There seems to be in the minds of men an instinctive awe of anything that appertains to the insane. In olden times a disordered mind was considered of divine or diabolic origin as it evinced good or evil tendencies. This belief lasted even until the present century. Many old women who were the victims of senile dementia and kindred ills, were accused of witchcraft and intercourse with the devil, here in the United States, not a century ago. Witches were executed in England and men burned at the stake in Spain, not two hundred years ago, for the crime of demoniacal possession. Even in this enlightened age men are accustomed to consider insanity rather from its psychical standpoint than from its physical aspect. They do not take into consideration the fact that insanity is due to a physical lesion, and that its vagaries are but the symptoms of brain disease or brain deformity. The inhabitants of the borderlands are invested with a certain shadowy mystery which separates them from the rest of mankind, and which makes them appear to us as denizens of another psychical world than ours.

In the Middle Ages, cranks, whose eccentricities took a religious turn, were considered holy. St. Simon Stylites was a very pronounced crank, and a very holy man also, because he chose to live the greater portion of his life perched on a pillar seventy feet high. St. Anthony was another holy crank who never, in all his life, washed his feet. Poor Joan of Arc was burned at the stake because she was "possessed of a false and lying devil." She has been recently proposed for canonization by the same church that burned her, and thus, in a measure, had justice done her. I do not think, however, that this is any recompense for the terrible agony inflicted on this unfortunate victim of hystero-epilepsy.

Says Maudsley in "Responsibility in Mental Disease": "Some of the prophets of the Old Testament presented symptoms which can hardly be interpreted as other than the effects of madness; certainly if they were not mad, they imitated very closely some of its most striking features." Jeremiah takes a long journey to the river Euphrates and hides a linen girdle in a hole of a rock. He then returns home and in a few days makes the same journey, and finds the girdle rotten and good for nothing. Ezekiel digs a hole in the wall of his house, and through it removes his household goods, instead of through the door. Hosea marries a prostitute because he said he had been commanded by God so to do. Isaiah stripped himself naked and paraded up and down in sight of all the people.

Some of the greatest changes in the world's history have been effected by dwellers in the borderlands. Mahomet was an epileptic, and his first vision was the result on an epileptic convulsion or seizure. The character of his visions was exactly like that of those visions which an epileptic sees and describes at the present time. Mahomet believed in his visions, and, what is more, got more than half the world to believe in them also. Gautama was a dweller in the borderlands, yet his followers now number five hundred millions.

The novel mode in which an insane man regards things may be an inspiration which reflection could never attain, and it sometimes happens that opinions which seem to the world to be the ravings of a madman, have turned out to be true. The insane man has the world against him, and though he may pose for a short time as a reformer, sooner or later lands in the asylum.

It sometimes happens that the crank will succeed in getting converts. A notable instance is Schweinfurth, or "the Christ," as he calls himself. I am firmly convinced that this man believes in his delusions. One thing is certain, and that is, his disciples believe in him implicitly. This man is dangerous to society, inasmuch as he has caused the separation of several wives from their husbands; the wives abandoning their husbands to follow him to "Heaven," as he calls his farm house.

The crank is, generally, a harmless individual, and is not anti-social unless his delusions take the form of homicidal impulse, pyromania, kleptomania, etc.

Homicidal impulse is the most dangerous to society of the many mental vagaries and derangements which afflict the dwellers in the borderlands. Its invasion is sudden and its impulse is, generally, overpowering. A man may be walking the streets presumably in perfect health, and yet have, all the while, a voice whispering in his ear "kill, kill." His insane desire at length reaches its acme, and he throws aside every mental restraint and kills the first individual he may chance to meet. Again, he may desire to kill some particular individual, and will carefully and systematically arrange his plans for the successful enactment of the homicide. The murderers of Garfield and Harrison probably belong to this latter class, though in the case of Prendergast, the slayer of Mayor Harrison, this opinion may be erroneous. There is something about his photograph that leads me to believe that he is a moral imbecile, rather than an intellectual dyscrasiac.

A clerk in a solicitor's office, at Alton, Hampshire, England, one afternoon took a walk outside the town, when he met some children. He persuaded one of these, a girl of nine, to go with him into a neighboring garden. A short while after, he was seen walking quietly home; he was seen to wash himself in the river and then go back to his office. The little girl did not return home, and, search having been instituted, her dismembered body was found strewn about the garden. The clerk was arrested, and in his diary was found this entry, recently made: "Killed a little girl; it was fine and hot." This man was either a sadistic sexual pervert, or a victim of homicidal impulse. Maudsley gives this instance as an example of the latter, while Krafft-Ebing gives it as an example of the former. There is a great difference between these two mental derangements. The victim of homicidal impulse kills without any ulterior object, while the sadist kills in order to gratify his unnatural and perverted sexual appetite.

The victim of homicidal impulse is, to all outward appearances, perfectly sane otherwise. His impulse frequently leaves him for years and then returns with overpowering force.

Epileptics who have just passed through violent convulsions, will frequently attack bystanders with great fury. Some alienists declare that homicidal mania is frequently only a masked epilepsy. All epileptics should be carefully watched; they may become dangerous to society at any moment. Numerous instances are recorded of murder committed by sufferers from *petit mal*, a form of epilepsy. I once saw a negro walk up to a white man, who was a stranger and unknown by him, and fell him to the earth by striking him with a club. The negro was arrested, and the next day swore that he was entirely unconscious of having struck anyone. It was proven at his trial that he was subject to mild epileptic attacks.

I believe that all suicides are due to mental aberration. It may be the result of a momentary and sudden loss of mental equipoise, or the final and fatal ending of a premeditated desire carried through days, weeks, months, and even years.

We see a man, blessed with everything that makes life enjoyable, genial, gay, with a ready smile and kindly word for everyone, suddenly, in a moment, pass forever out into the unknown—self-killed, a victim of his own creation. We stand amazed! Why did he do it? We can find nothing in his past or present condition to warrant such an action.

He was the victim of momentary aberration, or, perhaps, deep in his mind, buried and hidden even from himself, there dwelt a desire for self-slaughter, when a "physical pain, an unexpected impression, a moral affection, an indiscreet proposition" uncovered this desire, and he at once committed the deed!

There are epidemics of suicide. Let the papers chronicle some peculiar method of suicide selected by some unfortunate, and others will immediately follow his example. Unconscious cerebration also hurls many souls out of the world. I was called to see a gentleman who had attempted suicide by slashing the radial artery at the wrist. I found him holding a compress on the severed vessel and greatly alarmed. He swore to me that he was totally unconscious how he had come to do the deed, and that he did not know that he had cut himself until he felt the pain and saw the blood flowing from the wound!

Viraginity and effemination, while not mental insanities, strictly speaking, are, nevertheless, mental deformities, and their unfortunate victims are dwellers in the borderlands. Mild forms of these types of degeneration are very abundant. The effeminate, cigarette-smoking, soda-drinking young man of the comic weeklies, and the loud, horsy, slang-using, vulgar, masculine young woman are seen everywhere.

Effemination and viraginity are the results of the weakening effects of luxury and consequent debauchery. Nations, time and again, have felt the dire effects of effemination and have sunk beneath them. The Grecian, the Roman, the Egyptian nations are familiar examples. The satirists of the golden age of the Latin people dipped their *stili,* metaphorically, in gall and bitter wormwood and berated the effeminate nobility time and again. One of them advised the Roman ladies to look for *men* among the gladiators and the peasants! Anacreon's poems are filled with allusions to effemination and the delights of psychic hermaphroditism.

In the time of Louis XIV., of France, the royal palaces were filled to repletion with effeminants, who vied with the women in the splendor of their robes and the salacious eccentricities of their conduct. The case of Alice Mitchell, who killed Freda Ward in Memphis not long ago, was one of pronounced viraginity.

Fortunately, for the good of the community at large, there are, comparatively speaking, few viragints. The careful mother restrains, tempers, and abolishes the hoydenish habits of her "tom-boy" girl early in life, and turns her thoughts toward feminine pursuits and desires. The unfortunate effeminant, however, is encouraged in his feminine tastes and habits by his unwise mother, who likes her boy to sit beside her and sew and knit, if he so desires. She discusses matters of the toilet with him, and, in fact, treats him as she would a daughter. In the end, his psychic hermaphroditism becomes complete, and one more unfortunate goes out into the world to swell the ranks of crankdom!

Kleptomaniacs are greatly to be pitied, for they are generally women in whom the moral sense is very much developed. The victim of kleptomania will steal any and everything; they are like magpies in this respect. An acquaintance of mine, a most estimable lady, a devout Christian, and a most exemplary wife and mother, is the most incorrigible thief I ever saw. She has often picked my pockets while I was engaged about her sick-bed. The merchants of the city where she lives know her infirmity, watch her while she is in their shops, and respectfully and kindly relieve her of her pilferings when she starts to leave. She expresses great sorrow for her unfortunate insane impulse, and has often begged her husband to have her placed in an asylum. This he refuses to do, as she is perfectly sane otherwise. The husband was called away for several weeks, and, on his return, took me to his house and showed me her room. In the room were the objects stolen during his absence. It was the most miscellaneous collection of valuables and trash I ever saw. She had gathered together everything from a darning-needle to a tombstone, a small specimen of the latter forming a unit of this heterogeneous whole. This form of mental dyscrasia is much more frequent than people suppose, and the antecedents of shop-lifters and the like should be carefully examined before a judgment on their criminality is passed.

"Eccentricity is certainly not always insanity, but there can be no question that it is often the outcome of insane temperament, and may approach very near to, or actually pass into, insanity." Alienists rely on the eccentric and peculiar changes which take place in the characters of their patients, who either present themselves or are brought to them for treatment, to establish their diagnosis. If a modest and truthful man suddenly becomes a braggart and a liar; or, if a humane man becomes cruel, or a neat man slovenly, there is reason to suspect brain trouble. The intellect may appear intact, so also the reasoning powers, but these eccentricities indicate a deviation which may lead to mental destruction. The last faculty to develop in the mind of man is the moral faculty; this faculty is the one first lost by diseased brains. If a man, who suddenly becomes dissolute and licentious (who, heretofore, has led a virtuous, moral life), be examined, in nine cases in ten his brain will be found to be diseased. The little cloud, which at first is no larger than a man's hand, grows ever larger and larger, and in the end overspreads the entire mental sky!

GENIUS AND DEGENERATION.

That the psychical function or intellectuality is frequently developed at the expense of the physical organism is well known, and that genius is seldom or never unaccompanied by physical and mental degeneration is a fact that can be no longer denied. I use the word degeneration in its broadest sense, and intend it to include all kinds of abnormalities. The facts noted above are by no means recent knowledge, but were vaguely recognized and commented on centuries and decades of centuries ago by the Hebrews and kindred races of people. The Hebrew word *nabi* means either madman or prophet, and it is now admitted that most of the prophets gave evidences of insanity as well as genius. The Greeks and the Romans recognized this kinship, and we read in the Bible of a certain Festus, who, when confronted by a man of genius, and being unable to answer his arguments, said to him, "Paul, much learning hath made thee mad!" Lauvergne, when speaking of the oxycephalic (sugarloaf) skull, an unquestionable example of degeneration, wrote many years ago, "This head announces the monstrous alliance of the most eminent faculty of man, genius, with the most pronounced impulses to rape, murder, and theft."

The purpose of this paper is to show that wherever genius is observed, we find it accompanied by degeneration, which is evinced by physical abnormalties or mental eccentricities. It is a strange fact, however, and one not noticed by Lombroso, or any other writer, as far as I know, that mechanical geniuses, or those who, for the most part, deal with material facts, do not, as a rule, show any signs of degeneration. I have only to instance Darwin, Galileo, Edison, Watts, Rumsey, Howe, and Morse to prove the truth of this assertion. It is only the genius of æstheticism, the genius of the emotion, that is generally accompanied by unmistakable signs of degeneration.

Saul, the first king of Israel, was a man of genius and, at times, a madman. We read that, before his coronation, he was seized with an attack of madness and joined a company of kindred eccentrics. His friends and acquaintances were naturally surprised and exclaimed: "Is Saul among the prophets?" *i. e.*, "Has Saul become insane?" Again, we are told that he was suddenly seized with an attack of homicidal impulse, and tried to kill David. Before this time he had had repeated attacks of madness, which only the harp of David could control and subdue. David himself was a man whose mental equilibrium was not well established, as his history clearly indicates. He forsook his God, indulged in licentious practices, and was, withal, a very, immoral man at times. At his time, the Hebrews had reached a high degree of civilization. Abstract ethics had become very much developed, and any example of great immorality occurring during this epoch is proof positive of atavism or degeneration.

As I have intimated before, many of the ancient Hebrew prophets, who were unquestionably men of genius, gave evidences of insanity; notably Jeremiah, who made a long journey to the River Euphrates, where he hid a linen girdle. He returned home, and in a few days made the same journey and found the girdle rotten and good for nothing; Ezekiel, who dug a hole in the wall of his house, through which he removed his household goods, instead of through the door; Hosea, who married a prostitute, because God, so he declared, had told him so to do; and Isaiah, who stripped himself naked and paraded up and down in sight of all the people. King Solomon, a man of pre-eminent genius, was mentally unbalanced. The "Song of Solomon" shows very clearly that he was a victim of some psychical disorder, sexual in its character and origin. The poems of Anacreon are lascivious, lustful, and essentially carnal, and history informs us that he was a sexual pervert.

Swinburne's poems show clearly the mental bias of their author, who is described as being peculiar and eccentric. Many of the men of genius who have assisted in making the history of the world have been the victims of epilepsy. Julius Cæsar, military leader, statesman, politician, and author, was an epileptic. Twice on the field of battle he was stricken down by this disorder. On one occasion, while seated at the tribune, he was unable to rise when the senators, consuls, and prætors paid him a visit of ceremony and honor. They were offended at his seeming lack of respect, and retired, showing signs of anger. Cæsar returned home, stripped off his clothes, and offered his throat to be cut by anyone. He then explained his conduct to the senate, saying that he was the victim of a malady which, at times, rendered him incapable of standing. During the attacks of this disorder "he felt shocks in his limbs, became giddy, and at last lost consciousness." Molière was the victim of epilepsy; so also was Petrarch, Flaubert, Charles V., Handel, St. Paul, Peter the Great, and Dostoieffsky; Paganini, Mozart, Schiller, Alfieri, Pascal, Richelieu, Newton, and Swift were the victims of diseases epileptoid in character.

Many men of genius have suffered from spasmodic and choreic movements, notably Lenau, Montesquieu, Buffon, Dr. Johnson, Santeuil, Crébillon, Lombardini, Thomas Campbell, Carducci, Napoleon, and Socrates.

Suicide, essentially a symptom of mental disorder, has hurried many a man of genius out into the unknown. The list begins with such eminent men as Zeno, Cleanthes, Dionysius, Lucan, and Stilpo, and contains the names of such immortals as Chatterton, Blount, Haydon, Clive, and David.

Alcoholism and morphinism, or an uncontrollable desire for alcohol or opium in some form or other, are now recognized as evidences of degeneration. Men of genius, both in the Old World and in the New, have shown this form of degeneration. Says Lombroso: "Alexander died after having emptied ten times the goblet of Hercules, and it was, without doubt, in an alcoholic attack, while pursuing naked the infamous Thais, that he killed his dearest friend. Cæsar was often carried home intoxicated on the shoulders of his soldiers. Neither Socrates, nor Seneca, nor Alcibiades, nor Cato, nor Peter the Great (nor his wife Catherine, nor his daughter Elizabeth) were remarkable for their abstinence. One recalls Horace's line, *'Narratur et prisci Cantonis sæpe mero caluisse virtus.'* Tiberius Nero was called by the Romans Biberius Mero. Septimius Severus and Mahomet II. succumbed to drunkenness or *delirium tremens*."

Among the men and women of genius of the Old World who abused the use of alcohol and opium, were Coleridge, James Thomson, Carew, Sheridan, Steele, Addison, Hoffman, Charles Lamb, Madame de Staël, Burns, Savage, Alfred de Musset, Kleist, Caracci, Jan Steen, Morland Turner (the painter), Gérard de Nerval, Hartley Coleridge, Dussek, Handel, Glück, Praga, Rovani, and the poet Somerville. This list is by no means complete, as the well-informed reader may see at a glance; it serves to show, however, how very often this form of degeneration makes its appearance in men of genius.

In men of genius the moral sense is sometimes obtunded, if not altogether absent. Sallust, Seneca, and Bacon were suspected felons. Rousseau, Byron, Foscolo, and Caresa were grossly immoral, while Casanova, the gifted mathematician, was a common swindler. Murat, Rousseau, Clement, Diderot, Praga, and Oscar Wilde were sexual perverts.

Genius, like insanity, lives in a world of its own, hence we find few, if any, evidences of human affection in men of genius. Says Lombroso: "I have been able to observe men of genius when they had scarce reached the age of puberty; they did not manifest the deep aversions of moral insanity, but I have noticed among all a strange apathy for everything which does not concern them; as though, plunged in the hypnotic condition, they did not perceive the troubles of others, or even the most pressing needs of those who were dearest to them; if they observed them, they grew tender, at once hastening to attend them; but it was a fire of straw, soon extinguished, and it gave place to indifference and weariness."

This emotional anæsthesia is indicative of psychical atavism, and is an unmistakable evidence of degeneration. Lombroso gives a long list of the men of genius who were celibates. I will mention a few of those with whom the English-speaking world is most familiar: Kant, Newton, Pitt, Fox, Beethoven, Galileo, Descartes, Locke, Spinoza, Leibnitz, Gray, Dalton, Hume, Gibbon, Macaulay, Lamb, Bentham, Leonardo da Vinci, Copernicus, Reynolds, Handel, Mendelssohn, Meyerbeer, Schopenhauer, Camoëns, and Voltaire. La Bruyère says of men of genius: "These men have neither ancestors nor descendants; they themselves form their entire posterity."

There is a form of mental obliquity which the French term *folie du doute*. It is characterized by an incertitude in thought coördination, and often leads its victims into the perpetration of nonsensical and useless acts. Men of genius are very frequently afflicted with this form of mental disorder. Dr. Johnson, who was a sufferer from *folie du doute*, had to touch every post he passed. If he missed one he had to retrace his steps and touch it. Again, if he started out of a door on the wrong foot he would return and make another attempt, starting out on the foot which he considered the correct one to use. Napoleon counted and added up the rows of windows in every street through which he passed. A celebrated statesman, who is a personal friend of the writer, can never bear to place his feet on a crack in the pavement or floor. When walking he will carefully step over and beyond all cracks or crevices. This idiosyncracy annoys him greatly, but the impulse is imperative, and he can not resist it.

Those who have been intimately associated with men of genius have noticed that they are very frequently amnesic or "absent-minded." Newton once tried to stuff his niece's finger into the bowl of his lighted pipe, and Rovelle would lecture on some subject for hours at a time and then conclude by saying: "But this is one of my arcana, which I tell to no one." One of his students would then whisper what he had just said into his ear, and Rovelle would believe that his pupil "had discovered the arcanum by his own sagacity, and would beg him not to divulge what he himself had just told to two hundred persons."

Lombroso has combed history, as it were, with a fine-tooth comb, and very few geniuses have escaped his notice. This paper, so far, is hardly more than a review of his extraordinarily comprehensive work; therefore, I will conclude this portion of it with a list of men of genius, their professions, and their evidences of degeneration, as gathered from his book:

Carlo Dolce, painter, *religious monomania.*

Bacon, philosopher, *megalomania, moral anaesthesia.*

Balzac, writer, *masked epilepsy, megalomania.*

Cæsar, soldier, writer, *epilepsy.*

Beethoven, musician, *amnesia, melancholia.*

Cowper, writer, *melancholia.*

Chateaubriand, writer, *chorea.*

Alexander the Great, soldier, *alcoholism.*

Molière, dramatist, *epilepsy, phthisis pulmonalis.*

Lamb, writer, *alcoholism, melancholia, acute mania.*

Mozart, musician, *epilepsy, hallucinations.*

Heine, writer, *melancholia, spinal disease.*

Dr. Johnson, writer, *chorea, folie du doute.*

Malibran, *epilepsy.*

Newton, philosopher, *amnesia.*

Cavour, statesman, philosopher, *suicidal impulse.*

Ampère, mathematician, *amnesia.*

Thomas Campbell, writer, *chorea.*

Blake, painter, *hallucinations.*

Chopin, musician, *melancholia.*

Coleridge, writer, *alcoholism, morphinism.*

Donizetti, musician, *moral anaesthesia.*

Lenau, writer, *melancholia.*

Mahomet, theologian, *epilepsy.*

Manzoni, statesman, *folie du doute.*

Haller, writer, *hallucinations.*

Dupuytren, surgeon, *suicidal impulse.*

Paganini, musician, *epilepsy.*

Handel, musician, *epilepsy.*

Schiller, writer, *epilepsy.*

Richelieu, statesman, *epilepsy.*

Praga, writer, *alcoholism, sexual perversion.*

Tasso, writer, *alcoholism, melancholia.*

Savonarola, theologian, *hallucinations.*

Luther, theologian, *hallucinations.*

Schopenhauer, philosopher, *melancholia, omniphobia.*

Gogol, writer, *melancholia, tabes dorsalis.*

Lazaretti, theologian, *hallucinations.*

Mallarmé, writer, *suicidal impulse.*

Dostoieffsky, writer, *epilepsy.*

Napoleon, soldier, statesman, *folie du doute, epilepsy.*

Comte, philosopher, *hallucinations.*

Pascal, philosopher, *epilepsy.*

Poushkin, writer, *megalomania.*

Renan, philosopher, *folie du doute.*

Swift, writer, *paresis.*

Socrates, philosopher, *chorea.*

Schumann, musician, *paresis.*

Shelley, writer, *hallucinations.*

Bunyan, writer, *hallucinations.*

Swedenborg, theologian, *hallucinations.*

Loyola, theologian, *hallucinations.*

J. S. Mill, writer, *suicidal impulse.*

Linnæus, botanist, *paresis.*

The reader will observe that I have made use of the comprehensive word, writer, to designate all kinds of literary work except theology and philosophy. The above list is by no means complete, and only contains the names of those geniuses with whom the world is well acquainted.

When we come to the geniuses of the New World, we find that, though few in number, they, nevertheless, show erraticism and degeneration. Poe was undoubtedly a man of great genius, and his degeneration was indicated by his excessive use of alcohol. Aaron Burr was the victim of moral anæsthesia, and Jefferson was pseudo-epileptic and neurasthenic. Randolph was a man of marked eccentricity, and Benedict Arnold was, morally, anæsthetic. Daniel Webster was addicted to an over-indulgence in alcohol, likewise Thomas Marshall and the elder Booth. Booth also had attacks of acute mania. His son Edwin had paresis; so also had John McCullough, John T. Raymond, and Bartley Campbell. A distinguished statesman and politician, and a man who stands high in the councils of the nation, has, for a number of years, given evidence of mental obliquity by his uncontrollable desire for alcohol. No power, outside of bodily restraint, can control him and keep him from indulging his appetite for alcohol when this desire seizes him. One of the most noted poets of to-day, whose verses stir the heart with their pathos and bring smiles to the gravest countenances with their humor, was, for a number of years (and still is, so I have been told), an inordinate user of alcohol.

Robert Ingersoll was undoubtedly a man of genius and of considerable originality, and a close study of his writings shows conclusively his mental eccentricity. Judging wholly from his printed utterances, Mr. Ingersoll was only a superficial scientist and mediocre scholar. His power lay in his wonderful word imagery, and his intricately constructed verbal arabesques. He was a verbal symbolist. Symbolism, wherever found, and in whatever art, if carried to any extent, must necessarily be an evidence of atavism, consequently of degeneration.

Thomas Paine gave evidences of a lack of mental equipoise. We find scattered throughout his works the most brilliant, irrefutable, and logical truths side by side with the most inane, illogical, and stolid crudities. Among other men of genius who showed signs of degeneration we may include Alexander Stevens, Joel Hart, Adams, Train, Breckenridge,

Webster, Blaine, Van Buren, Houston, Grant, Hawthorne, Bartholow, Walt Whitman. We must not confound genius and talent—the two are widely different. Genius is essentially original and spontaneous, while talent is to some extent acquired. Genius is a *quasi* abnormality, and one for which the world should be devoutly grateful. *Psychos*, in the case of genius, is not uniformly developed, one part, being more favored than the others, absorbs and uses more than its share of that element, whatsoever it be, which goes to make up intellectuality, hence the less favored or less acquisitive parts show degeneration.

THE EFFECT OF FEMALE SUFFRAGE ON POSTERITY.

The greatest, best, and highest law of higher civilization is that which declares that man should strive to benefit, not himself alone, but his posterity.

I. THE ORIGIN OF THE MATRIARCHATE.

In the very beginning woman was, by function, a mother; by virtue of her surroundings, a housewife. Man was then, as now, the active, dominant factor in those affairs outside the immediate pale of the fireside. Life was collective; "communal was the habitation, and communal the wives with the children; the men pursued the same prey, and devoured it together after the manner of wolves; all felt, all thought, all acted in concert." Primitive men were like their simian ancestors, which never paired, and which roamed through the forest in bands and troops. This collectivism is plainly noticeable in certain races of primitive folks which are yet in existence, notably the autochthons of the Aleutian Islands. Huddled together in their communal *kachims*, naked, without any thought of immodesty, men, women, and children share the same fire and eat from the same pot. They recognize no immorality in the fact of the father cohabiting with his daughter—one of them naïvely remarking to Langsdorf, who reproached him for having committed this crime: "Why not? the otters do it!" Later in life the men and women mate; but even then there is no sanctity in the marriage tie, for the Aleutian will freely offer his wife to the stranger within his gates, and will consider it an insult if he refuses to enjoy her company. "As with many savages and half-civilized people, the man who would not offer his guest the hospitality of the conjugal couch, or the company of his best-looking daughter, would be considered an ill-bred person."

This laxity in sexual relations was, at first, common to all races of primitive men, but, after a time, there arose certain influences which modified, to a certain extent, this free and indiscriminate intercourse. Frequent wars must have occurred between hostile tribes of primitive men, during which, some of them (physically or numerically weaker than their opponents) must have been repeatedly vanquished, and many of their females captured, for, in those old days (like those of more recent times, for that matter) the women were the prizes for which the men fought.

Under circumstances like these, the few remaining women must have served as wives for all the men of the tribe; and, in this manner polyandry had its inception. Polyandry gives women certain privileges which monandry denies, and she is not slow to seize on these prerogatives, and to use them in the furtherance of her own welfare. Polyandry, originating from any cause whatever, will always end in the establishment of a matriarchate, in which the women are either directly or indirectly at the head of the government.

There are several matriarchates still extant in the world, and one of the best known, as well as the most advanced, as far as civilization and culture are concerned, is that of the Nairs, a people of India inhabiting that portion of the country lying between Cape Comorin and Mangalore, and the Ghâts and the Indian Ocean.

The Nairs are described as being the handsomest people in the world; the men being tall, sinewy and extraordinarily agile, while the women are slender and graceful, with perfectly modeled figures. The Nair girl is carefully chaperoned until she arrives at a marriageable age, say, fourteen or fifteen years, at which time some complaisant individual is selected, who goes through the marriage ceremony with her. As soon as the groom ties the *tali*, or marriage cord, about her neck, he is feasted and is then dismissed; the wife must never again speak to, or even look at, her husband. Once safely wedded, the girl becomes emancipated, and can receive the attentions of as many men as she may elect, though, I am informed, it is not considered fashionable, at present, to have more than seven husbands, one for each day of the week.

Of no importance heretofore, after her farcical marriage the Nair woman at once becomes a power in the councils of the nation; as a matter of course, the higher her lovers the higher her rank becomes and the greater her influence. Here is female suffrage in its primitive form, brought about, it is true, by environment, and not by elective franchise.

As far as the children are concerned, the power of the mother is absolute; for they know no father, the maternal uncle standing in his stead. Property, both personal and real, is vested in the woman; she is the mistress and the ruler. "The mother reigns and governs; she has her eldest daughter for prime minister in her household, through whom all orders are transmitted to her little world. Formerly, in grand ceremonials, the reigning prince himself yielded precedence to his eldest daughter, and, of course, recognized still more humbly the priority of his mother, before whom he did not venture to seat himself until she had given him permission. Such was the rule from the palace to the humblest dwelling of a Nair."

During the past fifty years, these people have made rapid strides toward civilization, monandry and monogamy taking the places of polyandry and polygamy, and fifty or a hundred years hence, this matriarchate will, in all probability, entirely disappear.

I have demonstrated, I think, clearly and distinctly, that matriarchy, or female government, is neither new nor advanced thought, but that it is as old, almost, as the human race; that the "New Woman" was born many thousands of years ago, and that her autotype, in some respects, is to be found to-day in Mangalore! A return to matriarchy at the present time would be distinctly and emphatically and essentially retrograde in every particular. The right to vote carries with it the right to hold office, and if women are granted the privilege of suffrage, they must also be given the right to govern. Now let us see if we cannot find a reason for this atavistic desire (matriarchy) in the physical and psychical histories of its foremost advocates. I will discuss this question in Part II of this paper.

II. THE VIRAGINT.

There are two kinds of genius. The first is progressive genius, which always enunciates new and original matter of material benefit to the human race, and which is, consequently, non-atavistic; the second is atavistic or retrogressive genius, which is imitative and which always enunciates dead and obsolete matter long since abandoned and thrown aside as being utterly useless. The doctrines of communism and of nihilism are the products of retrogressive genius and are clearly atavistic, inasmuch as they are a reversion to the mental habitudes of our savage ancestors. The doctrines of the matriarchate are likewise degenerate beliefs, and, if held by any civilized being of to-day, are evidences of psychic atavism.

Atavism invariably attacks the weak; and individuals of neurasthenic type are more frequently its victims than are any other class of people. Especially is this true in the case of those who suffer from psychical atavism.

The woman of to-day who believes in and inculcates the doctrines of matriarchy, doctrines which have been, as far as the civilized world is concerned, thrown aside and abandoned these many hundred years, is as much the victim of psychic atavism as was Alice Mitchell, who slew Freda Ward in Memphis several years ago, and who was justly declared a viragint by the court that tried her.

Without entering into the truthfulness or falseness of the theory advanced by me elsewhere in this book, in regard to the primal cause of psychic hermaphroditism, which I attributed and do still attribute to psychic atavism, I think that I am perfectly safe in asserting that every woman who has been at all prominent in advancing the cause of equal rights in its entirety, has either given evidences or masculo-femininity (viraginity), or has shown, conclusively, that she was the victim of psycho-sexual aberrancy. Moreover, the history of every viragint of any note in the history of the world shows that they were either physically or psychically degenerate, or both.

Jeanne d'Arc was the victim of hystero-epilepsy, while Catharine the Great was a dipsomaniac, and a creature of unbounded and inordinate sensuality. Messalina, the depraved wife of Claudius, a woman of masculine type, whose very form embodied and shadowed forth the regnant idea of her mind—absolute and utter rulership—was a woman of such gross carnality, that her lecherous conduct shocked even the depraved courtiers of her lewd and salacious court. The side-lights of history, as Douglas Campbell has so cleverly pointed out in his "Puritan in Holland, England, and America," declare that there is every reason to believe that the Virgin Queen, Elizabeth of England, was not such a pure and unspotted virgin as her admirers make her out to be. Sir Robert Cecil says of her that "she was more man than woman," while history shows conclusively that she was a pronounced viragint, with a slight tendency toward megalomania. In a recent letter to me, Mr. George H. Yeaman, ex-Minister to Denmark, writes as follows: "Whether it be the relation of cause and effect, or only what logicians call a "mere coincidence," the fact remains that in Rome, Russia, France, and England, political corruption, cruelty of government, sexual immorality—nay, downright, impudent, open, boastful indecency—have culminated, for the most part, in the eras of the influence of viragints on government or over governors."

Viraginity has many phases. We see a mild form of it in the tom-boy who abandons her dolls and female companions for the marbles and masculine sports of her boy acquaintances. In the loud-talking, long-stepping, slang-using young woman we see another form; while the square-shouldered, stolid, cold, unemotional, unfeminine android (for she has the normal human form, without the normal human *psychos*) is yet another. The most aggravated form of viraginity is that known as homo-sexuality; with this form, however, this paper has nothing to do.

Another form of viraginity is technically known as gynandry, and may be defined as follows: A victim of gynandry not only has the feelings and desires of a man, but also the skeletal form, features, voice, etc., so that the individual approaches the opposite sex anthropologically, and in more than a psycho-sexual way (Krafft-Ebing).

As it is probable that this form of viraginity is sometimes acquired to a certain extent, and that, too, very quickly, when a woman is placed among the proper surroundings, I shall give the case of Sarolta, Countess V., one of the most remarkable instances of gynandry on record. If this woman, when a child, had been treated as a girl, she would in all probability have gone through life as a woman, for she was born a female in every sense of the word. At a very early age, however, her father, who was an exceedingly eccentric nobleman, dressed her in boy's clothing, called her Sandor, and taught her boyish games and sports.

"Sarolta-Sandor remained under her father's influence till her twelfth year, and then came under the care of her maternal grandmother, in Dresden, by whom, when the masculine play became too obvious, she was placed in an institute and made to wear female attire. At thirteen she had a love relation with an English girl, to whom she represented herself as a boy, and ran away with her. She was finally returned to her mother, who could do nothing with her, and was forced to allow her to resume the name of Sandor and to put on boy's clothes. She accompanied her father on long journeys, always as a young gentleman; she became a *roué*, frequenting brothels and *cafés* and often becoming intoxicated. All of her sports were masculine; so were her tastes and so were her desires. She had many love affairs with women, always skillfully hiding the fact that she herself was a woman. She even carried her masquerade so far as to enter into matrimony with the daughter of a distinguished official and to live with her for some time before the imposition was discovered." The woman whom Sandor married is described as being "a girl of incredible simplicity and innocence;" in sooth, she must have been!

Notwithstanding this woman's passion for those of her own sex, she distinctly states that in her thirteenth year she experienced normal sexual desire. Her environments, however, had been those of a male instead of a female, consequently her psychical weakness, occasioned by degeneration inherited from an eccentric father, turned her into the gulf of viraginity, from which she at last emerged, a victim of complete gynandry. I have given this instance more prominence than it really deserves, simply because I wish to call attention to the fact that environment is one of the great factors in evolutionary development.

Many women of to-day who are in favor of female suffrage are influenced by a single idea; they have some great reform in view, such as the establishment of universal temperance, or the elevation of social morals. Suffrage in its entirety, that suffrage which will give them a share in the government, is not desired by them; they do not belong to the class of viragints, unsexed individuals, whose main object is the establishment of a matriarchate.

Woman is a creature of the emotions, of impulses, of sentiment, and of feeling; in her the logical faculty is subordinate. She is influenced by the object immediately in view, and does not hesitate to form a judgment which is based on no other grounds save those of intuition. Logical men look beyond the immediate effects of an action and predicate its results on posterity. The percepts and recepts which form the concept of equal rights also embody an eject which, though conjectural, is yet capable of logical demonstration, and which declares that the final and ultimate effect of female suffrage on posterity would be exceedingly harmful.

We have seen that the pronounced advocates and chief promoters of equal rights are probably viragints—individuals who plainly show that they are psychically abnormal; furthermore, we have seen that the abnormality is occasioned by degeneration, either acquired or inherent, in the individual. Now let us see, if the right of female suffrage were allowed, what effect it would produce on the present environment of the woman of to-day, and, if any, what effect this changed environment would have on the psychical habitudes of the woman of the future. This portion of the subject will be discussed in Part III of this paper.

III. The Decadence.

It is conceded that man completed his cycle of physical development many thousands of years ago. Since his evolution from his pithecoid ancestor the forces of nature have been at work evolving man's psychical being. Now, man's psychical being is intimately connected with, and dependent upon, his physical being; therefore it follows that degeneration of his physical organism will necessarily engender psychical degeneration also. Hence, if I can prove that woman, by leading a life in which her present environments are changed, produces physical degeneration, it will naturally follow that psychical degeneration will also accrue; and, since one of the invariable results of degeneration, both physical and psychical, is atavism, the phenomenon of a social revolution in which the present form of government will be overthrown and a matriarchate established in its stead, will be not a possibility of the future, but a probability.

That the leaders of this movement in favor of equal rights look for such a result, I have not the slightest doubt; for, not many days ago, Susan B. Anthony stood beside the chair of a circuit judge in one of our courthouses and, before taking her seat, remarked that there were those in her audience who doubtless thought "that she was guilty of presumption and usurpation" (in taking the judge's chair), but that there would come a day when they would no longer think so!

Statistics show clearly and conclusively that there is an alarming increase of suicide and insanity among women, and I attribute this wholly to the already changed environment of our women. As the matter stands they have already too much liberty. The restraining influences which formerly made woman peculiarly a housewife have been, in a measure, removed, and woman mixes freely with the world. Any new duty added to woman as a member of society would modify her environment to some extent and call for increased nervous activity. When a duty like suffrage is added the change in her environment must necessarily be marked and radical, with great demands for an increased activity. The right of suffrage would, unquestionably, very materially change the environment of woman at the present time, and would entail new and additional desires and emotions which would be other and most exhausting draughts on her nervous organism.

The effects of degeneration are slow in making their appearance, yet they are exceedingly certain. The longer woman lived amid surroundings calling for increased nervous expenditure, the greater would be the effects of the accruing degeneration on her posterity. "Periods of moral decadence in the life of a people are always contemporaneous with times of effeminacy, sensuality, and luxury. These conditions can only be conceived as occurring with increased demands on the nervous system, which must meet these requirements. As a result of increase of nervousness there is increase of sensuality, and since this leads to excess among the masses it undermines the foundations of society—the morality and purity of family life" (Krafft-Ebing).

The inherited psychical habitudes, handed down through hundreds and thousands of years, would prevent the immediate destruction of that ethical purity for which woman is noted, and in the possession of which she stands so far above man. I do not think that this ethical purity would be lost in a day or a year, or a hundred years, for that matter; yet there would come a time when the morality of to-day would be utterly lost, and society would sink into some such state of existence as we now find *en evidence* among the Nairs. In support of this proposition I have only to instance the doctrines promulgated by some of the most advanced advocates of equal rights. The "free love" of some advanced women, I take it, is but the free choice doctrine in vogue among the Nairs and kindred races of people.

John Noyes, of the Oneida Community, where equal rights were observed, preached the same doctrines. It is true that the people who advocate such unethical principles are degenerate individuals, psychical atavists, yet they faithfully foreshadow in their own persons that which would be common to all men and women at some time in the future, if equal rights were allowed, and carried out in their entirety.

This is an era of luxury, and it is a universally acknowledged fact that luxury is one of the prime factors in the production of degeneration. We see forms and phases of degeneration thickly scattered throughout all circles of society, in the plays which we see performed in our theaters, and in the books and papers published daily throughout the land. The greater portion of the *clientèle* of the alienist and neurologist is made up of women who are suffering with neurotic troubles, generally of a psychopathic nature. The number of viragints, gynandrists, androgynes, and other psycho-sexual aberrants of the feminine gender is very large indeed.

It is folly to deny the fact that the right of female suffrage will make no change in the environment of woman. The New Woman glories in the fact, that the era which she hopes to inaugurate will introduce her into a new world. Not satisfied with the liberty she now enjoys, and which is proving to be exceedingly harmful to her in more ways than one, she longs for more freedom, a broader field of action. If nature provided men and women with an inexhaustible supply of nervous energy, they might set aside physical laws, and burn the candle at both ends without any fear of its being burned up. Nature furnishes each individual with just so much nervous force and no more; moreover, she holds every one strictly accountable for every portion of nervous energy which he or she may squander; therefore, it behooves us to build our causeway with exceeding care, otherwise we will leave a chasm which will engulf posterity.

The baneful effects resulting from female suffrage will not be seen to-morrow, or next week, or week after next, or next month, or next year, or a hundred years hence, perhaps. It is not a question of our day and generation; it is a matter involving posterity. The simple right to vote carries with it no immediate danger, the danger comes afterward; probably many years after the establishment of female suffrage, when woman, owing to her increased degeneration, gives free rein to her atavistic tendencies, and hurries ever backward toward the savage state of her barbarian ancestors. I see, in the establishment of equal rights, the first step toward that abyss of immoral horrors so repugnant to our cultivated ethical tastes—the matriarchate. Sunk as low as this, civilized man will sink still lower—to the communal *kachims* of the Aleutian Islanders.

IS IT THE BEGINNING OF THE END?

When we come to examine the history of the world we find evidence that certain nations have, at times, reached a high state of prosperity, and have then degenerated to such a degree that they have either passed entirely out of existence, or have lapsed into a state of semi-barbarity. This has generally been brought about by conquest, but the races conquered had first become enfeebled by their habitudes of thought and manner of living. It is a well-established fact that luxury brings debauchery, and that debauchery occasions degeneration. All nations that have, heretofore, reached the zenith of their prosperity, have been engulfed, at some time or other, in the maelstrom of luxurious habits, and have fallen under the lethal influence of a degeneration occasioned solely by debauchery; for the luxury and debauchery of one class brought increased poverty on, as well as excess in, other classes, and poverty and excess are prominent factors in the production of degeneration, as we shall see further on in this paper. Says the brilliant author of "Psychopathia Sexualis," Krafft-Ebing: "Periods of moral decadence in the life of a people are always contemporaneous with times of effeminacy, sensuality, and luxury. These conditions can only be conceived as occurring with increased demands upon the nervous system, which must meet these requirements. As a result of increase of nervousness, there is increase of sensuality, and, since this leads to excesses among the masses, it undermines the foundations of society—the morality and purity of family life. When this is destroyed by excesses, unfaithfulness, and luxury, then the destruction of the state is inevitably compassed in material, moral, and political ruin."

Such was the condition of the Latin race when the fierce and hardy Vandals overran the Roman peninsula; such was the condition of the Assyrians when Babylon fell beneath the onslaughts of the great Macedonian; such was the condition of the Egyptians when the northern myriads swept down upon the fertile valley of the Nile, and destroyed forever the once powerful and all-conquering kingdom of the Pharaohs; and such, too, was the condition of the French nation in 1794, when Anarchy unfurled its red banner at the head of the most gigantic social revolution the world has ever known.

At the present time, community of interests, as well as higher civilization, would utterly forbid the total subjugation of one civilized nation by another, such as occurred in the olden times; hence no nation need fear annihilation from such a source. The danger comes from another point, and consists in the almost certain uprising, at some time in the future, of degenerate individuals in open warfare and rebellion against society.

The question whether the world is growing better or worse is often debated, and can be answered affirmatively on both sides. Better, because superstition, bigotry, and dogmatism have given way, to a great extent, to the tolerance and freedom of higher civilization and purer ethics in normal, healthy man; worse, because crime (and I mean by crime *all* anti-social acts) has greatly increased on account of the pernicious influence of degeneration.

That superstition, bigotry, and dogmatism are on the wane, and that they will, sooner or later, be entombed in that depository of obsolete savage mental habitudes—absolute and utter oblivion—a glance at the success that science has achieved in the warfare waged against it by the Church, will at once declare. (Throughout this article I use the word Church to express priests of any and every denomination, whether Jew, Gentile, or Pagan, Protestant or Catholic.) A short incursion into this subject, *i. e.*, the Church's warfare on science, is absolutely necessary. For the triumph of science over its enemies—superstition, bigotry, and dogmatism, coincidently, ignorance and illiterateness—shows that the civilized world, at the present time, is markedly different in some respects from the world of ancient, medieval, and even comparatively recent times; and, in summing up, this changed condition will be a weighty factor in making up an answer to the question which heads this paper.

When Olympus first faded away from the enlightened eyesight of the Greeks, and changed into space besprinkled with stars; when Zeus no longer held his divine court on its mystic summit; when oracles became mute and the fabled wonders of the "Odyssey" either vanished, or resolved themselves into prosaic commonplaces under the investigations of the skeptic or the accidental discoverer, the Church made a most strenuous protest against the destruction of its traditions.

Many of these early seekers after truth were even killed and their goods confiscated. The Church issued its edict against heresy (and any doctrine that taught a belief antagonistic to the accepted tenets of pagan mythology and theogony was heresy), and hurled its anathemas against the heretic. Olympus, in the eyes of the Church, still existed, and Zeus, the man-god, still quaffed the sacred ambrosia in its shady groves. The Sirens still sang their entrancing songs, while Scylla and Charybdis were ever stretching out eager arms toward unwary mariners. Gigantic one-eyed Cyclops, with Polyphemus as their leader, still patrolled the shores of Sicily, and kept their "ever-watchful eyes" turned toward the open sea.

The hardy Greek sailor landed on the Cyclopean island, and discovered that Polyphemus, and Arges, and Brontes, and Steropes, and all the other one-eyed monsters were nothing but sea-wrack, bowlders, and weeds. He sailed farther, past Scylla and Charybdis, and discovered no greater dangers than sharp rocks and whirlpools. Yet farther he sailed out into the unknown sea, and the only Siren's song he heard was the whistling of the wind through the cordage of his vessel.

In vain the Church thundered against the daring investigator. Neither fire, nor sword, nor imprisonment, nor death itself could check the march of truth. Mythology and pagan theogony had received their death-blows; superstition, bigotry, and dogmatism were elbowed aside and gave place to dawning science. The Church held that that which had been believed by pious men for untold ages must necessarily be true. Science, in the garb of philosophy, with cold, dispassionate criticism, proved that these hitherto accepted truths were arrant fallacies. The poets and writers then took up the subject, and finally the people fell into line, so superstitious, bigoted, dogmatic mythology died, intellectuality took its place, and higher civilization took a step forward.

Thomas H. Huxley writes, in his preface to "Science and Christian Tradition," as follows: "I have never 'gone out of my way' to attack the Bible or anything else; it was the dominant, ecclesiasticism of my early days, which, as I believe, without any warrant from the Bible itself, thrust the book in my way.

"I had set out on a journey, with no other purpose than that of exploring a certain province of natural knowledge; I strayed no hair's breadth from the course which it was my right and my duty to pursue; and yet I found that, whatever route I took, before long I came to a tall and formidable looking fence. Confident as I might be in the existence of an ancient and indefeasible right of way, before me stood the thorny barrier with its comminatory notice-board—'No THOROUGHFARE. By order. MOSES.' There seemed no way over; nor did the prospect of creeping round, as I saw some do attract me… The only alternatives were either to give up my journey—which I was not minded to do—or to break the fence down and go through it."

Huxley found that this Mosaic fence, as erected by dogmatic theologians and scholasticists, was but a flimsy structure at best, and one that was easily overthrown and destroyed.

Dogmatic theology teaches that man was created from the dust of the earth, and that he at once fell heir to an estate of physical and psychical habitudes which were God-like in character; scientific investigation, on the contrary, demonstrated the fact that man's inception begins in bathybian protoplasm and culminates, as far as his general physical organism is concerned, in the last link of an evolutionary chain that reaches back and back, through countless eons of ages, to the very beginnings of life.

The History of Life written upon the rocky frame-work of this gray and hoary old world, declares that man's physical being is but the result of the laws of evolution. He did not spring into being, like the sea-born Venus, a creature of physical grace, and strength, and beauty; nor did the sacred flame of an inborn intelligence at once illumine his countenance. For thousands of years, the forbears of the present civilized *homo sapiens* were but slightly above the *Alalus* (ape-like man) of Haeckel in point of personal pulchritude; and for thousands of years, the ancestors of the civilized man of to-day were savages, with all the psychical traits of primitive peoples.

Social ethics are as much the result of evolutionary growth as is man himself. Civilization, which is but another name for ethical culture, is the outcome of the inherited experiences of thousands of years. These experiences were the results of law, and that law can be embraced in one comprehensive word—evolution.

Now, one of the most noticeable facts in biological history is the tendency that animal structures or organisms, under certain circumstances, have toward atavism or reversion to ancestral types. Not only is this to be observed in the physical organisms of animals, but also in their psychical beings as well.

Atavism is invariably the result of degeneration, as I will endeavor to demonstrate later on in this paper.

I believe that we are rapidly hurrying toward a social cataclysm, beside which the downfall of the Roman Empire, the destruction of ancient Egyptian and Babylonian civilizations, and the bloody days of the French Revolution will sink into utter insignificance. I believe, also, and think that I can demonstrate the truthfulness of my belief, that the inciting cause of this social revolution will not be found in those citizens of the United States of Anglo-Saxon and Celtic parentage, but that it will be observed among our Slavonic, Teutonic, and Latinic citizens. But, in order to furnish a parallel (from which you may draw your own conclusions), before I enter fully into the discussion of this part of my subject, I wish to review, very briefly, certain historical epochs.

When the first conquerors of Egypt, about whom history can tell us so little, first occupied the fertile valley of the Nile, the country, in all probability, was inhabited by negroes. The conquering race drove out or enslaved the native population and founded the ancient kingdom of Egypt. This kingdom waxed strong and mighty until, at the time of Rameses the Great, more than three thousand two hundred years ago, it was the most powerful monarchy in the whole world. The mighty son of Ra, Meiamoun Ra, or Rameses, as he is most generally styled, was a warrior and a statesman. He led his victorious troops north, east, and west, conquering nations as he went, until he dominated and brought into a state of vassalage over two-thirds of the then known world.

Wealth flowed into his kingdom from all the surrounding countries, consequently, luxury, with its never-failing associate, debauchery, made its appearance, and the decadence of this mighty kingdom set in.

It is true that many Pharaohs reigned after Rameses, and that the monarchy maintained its greatness for a long period of time, but luxury had taken hold on the Egyptians at the time of their greatest prosperity and had sown the seeds of degeneration, which flourished and grew apace, until the emasculated and effeminate people yielded up their independence to the conquerors, and passed out of existence as a nation forever.

The Roman people, under the leadership of their ancient heroes, was a nation of hardy warriors and husbandmen. That preëminent military genius, Julius Cæsar, had carefully fostered this warlike spirit in the bosoms of his compatriots, and, by a series of brilliant campaigns, had made the Roman nation the most powerful on the face of the globe. The Roman legions were not only victorious on land, extending their conquests into Iberia, farther Gaul, and still farther Britain, but the Roman triremes also swept the Mediterranean, from the Pillars of Hercules to the shores of Syria and Egypt. Wealth poured into the country from all sides, and the people reveled in a boundless prosperity.

Luxury had already begun to enervate the hardy soldiery at the time of Cæsar's assassination, yet not enough to show the full effects of degeneration and demoralization. The empire under the first emperors steadily grew richer and more powerful, and the luxury of the rich more unlimited and licentious. At length a change can be noticed. The Roman legions, hitherto victorious over every foe, are now frequently vanquished; conquered tribes uprear the standard of revolt and refuse to pay tribute; the territorial boundaries of the empire materially shrink, and its once conquered provinces pass out of its dominion forever.

The gradual degeneration of this nation is faithfully mirrored in the character of the emperors who governed it. Nero, Caligula, Tiberius, Caracalla, and Messalina, the depraved wife of Claudius and the daughter of Domitia Lepida, herself a licentious and libidinous woman, were but accentuated types of the luxurious and debauched nobility. Not only did the nobility become victims of degeneration, but the poorer classes also lost their virility, until at last we find the stability of the nation preserved through the instrumentality of foreign mercenaries. The greatness of this once widespread empire dwindled away (the freedom of its institutions contracting along with its shrinking boundaries), until we find it lapsed into a state of barbarian despotism under the son of Aurelius; and, had it not been for outside influences, it would have eventually fallen into a state of utter and complete savagery.

Now let us turn to a recent civilization. At the time of Louis XVI., the French nation was thoroughly under the influence of degeneration consequent to a luxury and licentiousness that had had a cumulative action for several hundred years. The peasantry and the inhabitants of the faubourgs, owing to their extreme poverty, itself a powerful factor in the production of degeneration, had lapsed into a state closely akin to that of their savage ancestors. The nobility were weak and effeminate, the majority of them either sexual perverts or monsters of sensuality and lechery.

The middle class, as ever the true conservators of society, seeing this miserable state of affairs, attempted to remedy it. Not fully understanding the danger of such a procedure, they allowed the degenerate element to share in their deliberations. Their moderate and sensible counsels were quickly overruled by their savage associates, who brought about a Reign of Terror (with such psychical atavists as Marat, Danton, and Robespierre at its head), the like of which the world had never seen before, nor has ever experienced since.

I have demonstrated, in the three instances of history just cited, that degeneration has invariably followed luxury, and that a social and political cataclysm has been, invariably, the result of this degeneration. That certain classes of the Old World, and of the New World, also, are living in inordinate luxury; and that certain other classes are, even now, struggling in the very depths of poverty, is a well-known fact. That this state of affairs is rapidly increasing the percentage of degenerates, such as sexual perverts, insane individuals, and congenital criminals, is not generally known; yet it is a woeful truth.

The factors in the production of degeneration are as multitudinous as they are varied, and I can find space for only a few of them. The artificiality of many peoples' lives, wherein night is turned into day, is a prominent factor in the production of degeneration. Now, the long continued influence of artificial light exerts a very deleterious effect on the nervous system; hence it is not to be wondered at that so many men and women of society are neurasthenic. Not only are those individuals who, voluntarily and preferably, spend the greater portions of their lives in artificial light, rendered nervously irritable, but those, also, who are driven by force of circumstances to turn night into day are likewise afflicted. Several years ago, I met a distinguished editor at Waukesha, who was suffering greatly from nervous exhaustion. He told me that he was so situated that he did all of his work at night, often writing until three o'clock in the morning. I advised him to quit this and to do his editorial work during daylight. Not long after, he wrote me that he had followed my advice, and that he was a new man in point of health.

The loss of nervous vitality makes itself evident by a feeling either of exhaustion or irritability. The fashionable devotee, in order to counteract this, either stimulates the system with alcohol, or exorcises the "fidgets" by the use of sedatives, such as chloral or morphia. The baneful effects of such medication are not at once appreciable, but, if continued for any length of time, they will eventually result in a total demoralization of the nervous system. Time and again have I seen fashionable men and women, at the close of the season, veritable nervous wrecks.

What necessarily would be the effect of physical and psychical lesions like these on a child begotten by such parents? The inevitable result would be degeneration in some form or other.

Again, many men and women stand the drain of a fashionable season on their nervous systems without attempting to recoup through the agency of drugs, and at the end find themselves physically and psychically exhausted. They go to the seaside or some other resort, and, in a measure, recover their nervous vitality, only to lose it again during the next season. This continues for season after season, the nervous system all the time becoming weaker, until some day there is a collapse, ending in hysteria, paresis, or some other of the hundred forms of neurotic disorder. What will be the effect on the progeny resulting from the union of such individuals? Again the answer must necessarily be—degeneration.

The long and continued intercourse of the sexes in the ball-room, where the women are dressed so *décolleté* that they excite sensuality in the men, very frequently without the men being conscious of the fact, must necessarily exert a deleterious effect on the nervous system.

Contact of the sexes in the dance is only pleasurable because of that contact. I am fully aware of the fact that this idea is scouted and denied by those who indulge in the waltz and kindred dances. They claim that no thought of carnality ever enters into their feelings. I know from personal experiences that they are honest in this declaration, yet, from a psychical standpoint, they are woefully in error. Aestheticism and carnality are by no means as dissociate as the æsthete would have us believe. *All pleasurable emotions that have their inception in the senses are, fundamentally, of carnal origin.* The waltz is æsthetic, yet all of its pleasure is based on an emotion closely akin to sensuality. Men derive no pleasure from waltzing with one another, nor do women under like circumstances.

Nature demands in the interest of health a certain amount of exercise. The luxurious society man or woman utterly disregards this demand of nature, consequently indigestion, with all of its associated ills, steps in, and becomes an additional factor in the production of nervous exhaustion. To tempt the appetite, highly seasoned foods, many of which are deleterious and injurious, are prepared and taken into the torpid and crippled stomach. Finally nature rebels and the unfortunate dyspeptic is forced to go through life on a diet of oatmeal, or, weakened by lack of healthy sustenance, the brain gives way, and the victim passes the remainder of his or her life in a lunatic asylum. Children begotten by miserable invalids like these, beyond a peradventure, must necessarily be degenerate.

Indigestion is not the only ill that nature inflicts for any disregard of her laws. She is a rough nurse but a safe one, consequently she forbids the rearing of her hardiest creation, man, in hot houses, as though he were a tender exotic. The luxurious individual pampers his body, following the dictates of his own selfish desires and utterly disregarding the laws of nature, and before he reaches middle age, discovers that he has become an old, old man, weak in body, but still weaker in mind.

The children resulting from the union of the various neurasthenics described above are necessarily degenerate. As they grow up, they show this degeneration by engaging in all kinds of licentious debauchery, and unnatural and perverted indulgences of appetite. In nine cases out of ten, they will spend the fortunes inherited from their parents in riotous debauchery, and will eventually sink, if death does not overtake them, to the level of their fellow degenerates—those who have been brought into existence by poverty and debauchery, and who await them at the foot of the social ladder. Among such degenerate beings, the doctrines of socialism, of communism, of nihilism, and of anarchy have their origin.

Now let us turn our attention to the evidences of luxury and debauchery, and the consequent evidences of degeneration, which obtrude themselves on all sides. The reckless extravagance of the nobility of the Old World is well known. Vice and licentiousness even penetrate to royal households, and princes of the blood pose as roués and debauchees. As I have demonstrated elsewhere, degeneration in the wealthy classes of society generally makes itself evident by the appearance of psycho-sexual disorders. The horrible abominations of the English nobility, as portrayed in the revelations of Mr. Stead, are well known. Charcot, Segalâs, Féré, and Bouvier give clear and succinct accounts of the vast amount of sexual perversion existing among the French, while Krafft-Ebing informs us that the German empire is cursed by the presence of thousands of these unfortunates. When we come to examine this phase of degeneration in our own country, we find that it is very prevalent. This is especially noticeable in the larger cities, though we find examples of it scattered broadcast throughout the land.

The editor of one of our leading magazines, in a remarkable series of letters, has shown that the wealthy New Yorkers revel in a luxuriousness that is absolutely startling in its license. Thousands are expended on a single banquet, while the flower bills for a single year of some of these modern Luculli would support a family of five people for three or four years! Bacchanalian orgies that dim even those of the depraved, corrupt, and degenerate Nero are of nightly occurrence.[A1] Drunkenness, lechery, and gambling are the sports and pastimes of these ultra rich men, and it is even whispered that milady is not much behind milord in the pursuit of forbidden pleasures.

Psycho-sexual disorders are not the only evidences of degeneration in the wealthy, by any means. Many a congenital criminal is born in the purple, who shows his moral imbecility in many ways. Sometimes he sinks at once to the level of a common thief, but generally his education keeps him within the pale of the law. Always, however, his sensuality is unbounded, and he will hesitate at nothing in order to gratify his desires. This unbridled license has already had its effect elsewhere. We see that it has even corrupted the guardians and conservators of the public peace. The recent investigation of the police board of New York shows a degree of corruption that is simply overwhelming, and that the same state of affairs exists in Chicago, New Orleans, St. Louis, and other large cities, I have every reason to believe.

There are yet other evidences of degeneration; witness the eroticism that is to be found in our literature. Unless a book appeals to the degenerate tastes of its readers it might just as well never have been published. This is not cynicism; it is plain, unvarnished truth. Again, turn to the stage, and we find the same thing. The tragedies and comedies of Shakespeare are shelved, while immoral "society plays" and "living pictures" and "problem plays" hold the boards. Salacity, with only sufficient and that is, degeneration. That which happened centuries ago will happen again, for covering to hide downright lewdness, is everywhere apparent. Now what is the result of this? There can be but one answer, man is governed by the same laws of nature now as he was then.

Statistics show that insanity is markedly on the increase. This is not to be wondered at when we take into consideration the fact that debauchery is the rule, and not the exception, among certain classes of people. Syphilis, one of the most productive causes of degeneration, is exceedingly active throughout the whole civilized world. Blashko states that one out of every ten men in the city of Berlin is tainted with this terrible malady. This is wholly attributable to the unbounded sensuality of the people. Crime of every description is rearing its hydra-head, and clasping in its destroying embrace an alarming proportion of human beings.

I have shown elsewhere, that the congenital criminal is the result of degeneration, and that he comes from all classes of society. He is, however, most frequently the product of the lower classes, and lives and dies among his congeners. I have shown, also, that the anarchist, the nihilist, and the socialist belong to the same category of degenerate beings. Poverty, brought on by high taxation, by war, and by overcrowding, has been, during the last millenary period, very fertile in the production of degenerates in the Old World. Lack of food and sanitation, the usual adjuncts of poverty, are powerful factors in the production of degenerate individuals. The Old World has gotten rid of these people as rapidly as possible by unloading them on our shores. Year after year, practically without restriction, thousands of these anti-social men and women have swarmed into our country, until we, comparatively speaking, a nation just born, contain as many of these undesirable citizens as any of the older nations. They still continue to enter our gates, and we ourselves are adding to their number, as I have shown, by our own production.

Some day—and I greatly fear that day is not very far distant—some professional anarchist (for there are professional anarchists as well as professional thieves) will consider the time ripe for rebellion, and, raising the fraudulent cry of "Labor against Capital!" instead of his legitimate cry of "Rapine! Murder! Booty!" will lead this army of degenerates, composed of anarchists, nihilists, sexual perverts, and congenital criminals, against society. And who will bear the brunt of this savage irruption? The ultra-rich? By no means! The great "middle class"—the true conservators of society and civilization—will fight this battle. It will be a fight between civilization and degeneration, and civilization will carry the day. There would have been no French revolution had the middle class been as wise then as it is to-day. It was taken by surprise at that savage, bloody time, but as soon as it recovered, how quickly it brought order out of chaos!

Education is the bulwark of civilization, and the great middle class, freed of dogmatism, bigotry, and superstition, is welcoming education with outstretched hands. It is gaining recruits, and is strengthening its defenses, so that when the time comes its enemies may find it fully prepared.

From the signs of the times and the evidence before me, I have no hesitation in declaring that I believe that the beginning of the end is at hand! This social cataclysm may not occur for many years, yet the agencies through which it will finally be evolved are even now at work, and are bringing the culmination of their labors ever nearer and nearer as time passes!

www.ingramcontent.com/pod-product-compliance
Lightning Source LLC
Chambersburg PA
CBHW081625100526
44590CB00021B/3599